P9-AFV-086

I   ES

COMMUNITY COLLEGE

ENESS

and Associates

rth Carolina State
lleges

ollege

ue
06

eges
ucation

America

DEMCO

CONTENTS

FOREWORD

Community college literature is replete with observations of the educational scene. Regardless of conditions or locations, key executives in our nation's community colleges are linked by many common dreams. They are also linked in a massive network demanding highly developed leadership, competency, and management skills. Their dreams and demands are primary in shaping the mission and fabric of our movement. It is their leadership that will significantly impact the future of the community colleges in America.

Leadership Strategies for Community College Effectiveness presents an overview of what we face in finance, demography, technology, governance, and curriculum. It focuses on our issues and targets our future.

The report of the Carnegie-supported Commission on Strengthening Presidential Leadership concludes by pointing out: "Strengthening presidential leadership is one of the most urgent concerns on the agenda of higher education in the United States. It makes a difference who the presidents are and what the conditions are that surround their contributions."

Community college administration has become a profession. The Presidents Academy of the American Association of Community and Junior Colleges has made a commitment to professionalism in this arena.

Programs and literature that present community college characteristics and needs are imperative in establishing and undergirding the foundation for our future. This volume presents an array of concerns and solutions related to the closing decades of this century and contributes significantly to our literature.

Leadership Strategies for Community College Effectiveness takes the lead in expressing commitment, provides stimulation for professionalism and leadership, and calls for dedication and courage.

Bernard J. Luskin
Executive Vice President
American Association of
Community and Junior Colleges

i

Preface

An open letter to Community College Leaders:

Are you . . .

- concerned that your curriculum programs are preparing graduates for obsolescence?
- asked to do more with less?
- experiencing new stiff competition?
- at a loss on how to keep your faculty—and yourself—abreast of the newest technologies?

All of you can identify with at least some of these challenges. According to Cohen,[1] some of you are trying to ignore the questions hoping that you are doing about as well as anyone else. Some of you shift the burden to someone else—send it to the curriculum committee or appoint a new task force. Some of you ask your colleagues how they have dealt with similar problems. A few even reach a point where you admit that you need a fresh perspective and ask for help. This book provides an overview of what one group of presidents were exposed to in seeking to acquire some new skills to maximize their leadership effectiveness in addressing many of these same challenges. Take some time and determine whether their findings have any applicability to you and your institution.

DATELINE: *Newsweek,* October 18, 1982: North Carolina's success in attracting high technology industries and matching skills to jobs is highlighted as a possible model to "Put America Back to Work." North Carolina's 58-campus community college system is nationally known for its strong commitment to technical education. The institutions play an important role in the sun belt state's efforts to shift its traditionally agriculture and manufacturing economy to a more diversified high technology, information-service economy. Obviously they have an excellent advantage compared to many states. But despite the nationwide acclaim, many North Carolina chief executives readily admit they are ill-prepared to provide effective leadership with the rapid changes occurring in today's technological society. Times have changed.

The two decades between the mid-'50s and mid-'70s have been called the "golden age" of higher education in America . . . a period characterized by growth and prosperity. This growth was particularly dramatic for the community college system, with a new two-year college established, on the average, every two weeks to meet the demands of unprecedented enrollment. Professional community college leadership programs during this period prepared administrators to be starters, creators, builders. The Department of Adult and Community College Education of North Carolina State University prepared approximately 30 such chief executives—many of whom were the early builders of the system—and who today face new challenges in a system in which not only the finances and the

---

[1]Arthur M. Cohen, "Foreward," In *Issues for Community College Leaders in a New Era,* ed. George B. Vaughan, (San Francisco: Jossey-Bass, 1983): ix.

number of students are changing sharply, but also the composition of the entire clientele, kinds of courses and programs wanted and schedules for them, the degree of competitiveness among colleges, the technology needed on campus, nature of the faculty, and the growing extent of external control and regulations. George Keller goes so far as to state "that the kind of management higher education needs does not exist yet. . ."[2]

Community college presidents turned to N.C. State for help in acquiring new skills needed to cope effectively with these new challenges. In response, the Department of Adult and Community College Education at N.C. State developed a proposal in cooperation with its general advisory committee for a pilot Community College Presidents' Leadership Institute. The proposal was endorsed by the North Carolina Association of Public Community College Presidents and the Chairman, North Carolina Association of Community College Trustees, and was adopted by the State Board of Community Colleges in the fall of 1983.

The primary goal of the project was to provide an intensive postdoctoral leadership renewal experience for North Carolina community college presidents conducting occupational education programs in the emerging technologies. A secondary goal was to record and disseminate appropriate segments of the activities of the institute and make it available to further enhance the leadership development of mid-level management of the nation's community, technical and junior colleges.

Significance of the Problem

The problem of the lack of effective leadership has significant educational and social implications. Sven Groennings, director, Fund for the Improvement of Post Secondary Education, stated at the 1981 Project Directors' Conference, "When education lags, the nation's ability to adapt, to progress and to compete is impeded. The greater the rate of change in technology and the world around us, the more and the faster education needs to adapt."

By the year 2000 in North Carolina over 35,000 jobs will be lost in the traditional industries of textiles, tobacco, food, wood and apparels. Over 149,000 new jobs are projected in instruments, metals, chemical, electrical, etc. (North Carolina Department of Administration). Nationwide the picture is similar as the biggest future job growth will be in the information service-related occupations which require skilled technical training (Bureau of Statistics). Community college leadership requires renewal of their skills to make informed decisions on critical resource allocations during this period of budget reversions in many states. A recent study by Ellen Chaffee[3], National Center for Higher Education Management Systems, found that the ability of the chief executive to focus the academic program (i.e., leadership) was a significant factor between recovering and non-recovering colleges that had experienced rapid financial decline. More importantly, maximizing leadership effectiveness can result in learner-centered improvements. Astin and Scherrei[4] concluded in a forty-nine private college and university

---

[2]George Keller, *Academic Strategy: The Management Revolution in American Higher Education*, (Baltimore: John Hopkins University Press, 1983).

[3]Ellen E. Chaffee, *Turnaround Management Strategies: The Adaptive Model and the Constructive Model*, unpublished draft report, Boulder, Colorado: National Center for Higher Education Management Systems, March 1983.

[4]Alexander W. Astin and Rita A. Scherrei, *Maximizing Leadership Effectiveness*, (San Francisco: Jossey-Bass Publishers, 1980): 114.

study that ten of twenty-four student outcome measures proved to be significantly correlated with one or more measures of presidential administrative type. During this period of rapid technological change, effective leadership is required in order to ensure that the community college system provides relevant, quality technical education to enable citizens to function in a rapidly changing job market.

Objectives

Objectives of the institute were as follows:
1. To enhance the capacity of institutions to plan strategically and utilize appropriate forms of new technology.
2. To enhance understanding of new management tools and new organizational forms that improve institutional management and decision making.
3. To strengthen the partnership between trustees and the chief executive to further enhance the institution's capability to communicate its mission to its constituencies.
4. To increase understanding of the role of organizational development in further enhancing institutional productivity and promoting quality educational programs.
5. To acquire new skills and strategies for updating community college occupational programs for the emerging technologies.
6. To acquire new skills and strategies in resource development, marketing and forming new partnerships with business and industry.
7. To enhance skills to effectively evaluate the impact of college on the learner, community and business constituencies.

Program Format and Resources

A modified version of Havelock's action model of organizational development was utilized in the institute.[5] For purposes of this project, action research was defined as the collaboration of researcher and practitioner in the diagnosis and evaluation of existing problems in the practice setting.

Prominent researchers and noted presidential practitioners were teamed to discuss both theory and practical experience with the participants. Dr. Byron McClenney, then Chairman, Presidents' Academy, American Association of Community and Junior Colleges, assisted in identifying chief executives from the academy to serve in the practitioner roles. Professors of community college education from the Council of Universities and Colleges, AACJC, were selected to synthesize current and emerging research.

The institute was organized into seven three-day sessions conducted at different host campuses across North Carolina. Case studies and active group involvement augmented lectures and seminars. The format provided the participating chief executives an opportunity to compare current research and practice and its applicability to their own operations as a mechanism for self-evaluation.

A Mid-Management Task Force was commissioned to assist in preparing the outcomes of the institute and provide their interpretations on the implications for leadership. Task force members are practicing professionals in the subject area they were asked to review and are pursuing their graduate program in Adult and Comunity College Education at North Carolina State University. Members were

---

[5]R. G. Havelock, *Planning for Innovation through Dissemination and Utilization of Knowledge,* (Ann Arbor, MI.: Institute for Social Research, University of Michigan, 1969).

charged to (1) review the tapes and support materials from their respective sessions and synthesize the principal resource persons' remarks; and (2) go beyond the sessions where necessary in drawing upon additional references in providing their reactions to the implications for leadership. As current and future leaders in the community college these task force members will be instrumental in deciding the future of their respective institutions. Testimony to this fact is that of the ten persons selected by the project director to serve on the task force, four of them received promotions at their respective colleges while working on the project. Manuscripts were in turn reviewed by the project director and the principal resource persons to ensure technical accuracy, consistency in editorial style, while attempting to convey the uniqueness of each individual's contribution and the style of the resource persons who collaborated on the institute. This volume is the culmination of this endeavor.

Limitations

1. The institute was specifically designed to meet the perceived needs of the chief executives of North Carolina community colleges. Presidents in the 58-campus community college system have a strong commitment to technical education and would be typically classified as heading small rural colleges whose growth enrollment trends currently range from slow to moderate growth with a slight overall decline for the system projected over the next five years. The institutions are formula funded (FTE) with strong to moderate state control in a sun belt, non-collective bargaining state.

2. The relevancy of the topics and resource persons selected for the institute were limited by the accuracy of the perceptions of the twelve-member advisory committee, composed of chief executives from the system and the project director.

3. The Mid-Management Task Force's review of the implications for leadership is limited to the extent of their experience bases and the fullness of their graduate education experience.

4. The applicability of the material to the reader will be dependent upon his or her ability to transfer and apply the concepts presented to his or her own setting.

Despite these limitations, the authors are confident that the material presented can assist other professionals in enhancing the skills and knowledge required to be successful leaders in this new era.

Cameron states that institutions in postindustrial environments must develop what he styles as Janusian characteristics where two contradictory thoughts are held true simultaneously. He maintains that institutions will need to be stable and at the same time flexible . . ." Initiating both continuity and change in leadership, specialization and generalization, proactivity and reactivity, and other seemingly contradictory chatacteristics will produce the adaptability necessary for effective higher education institutions in the future."[6]

What follows in this volume is a synthesis of thoughts of some of the best minds in community college education today who have and will continue to play significant roles in charting the course of the community college movement. Noted members of the professoriate and the presidents' academy are teamed in

[6]Kim S. Cameron, "Organizational Adaptation and Higher Education." *Journal of Higher Education* 55, no. 2 (March/April 1984): 137.

the following chapters in their own form of Janusian thinking. The chapters seek to synthesize the best of theory and sharing of successful practices of adaptive strategies to enhance community college effectiveness, which in this volume is defined as, making good on our promise of achieving opportunity with excellence.

Acknowledgements

I wish to extend my appreciation to the many people who made the project and this volume possible:

- Community College Education Advisory Committee, Department of Adult and Community College Education, North Carolina State University: David E. Daniel, President, Wilkes Community College; Clyde A. Erwin, Jr., President, Wayne Community College; Ben E. Fountain, Jr., President, Isothermal Community College; James L. Henderson, Jr., President, Coastal Carolina Community College; Bruce I. Howell, President, Wake Technical College; Dan W. Moore, President, Southeastern Community College; Joseph H. Nanney, President, Haywood Technical College; James A. Richardson, President, Western Piedmont Community College; Robert W. Scott, State President, North Carolina Department of Community Colleges; Louis Shields, Past President, North Carolina Association of Community College Trustees; Kathryn Baker Smith, Assistant to the State President for Policy Affairs, North Carolina Department of Community Colleges; Edward H. Wilson, Jr., Executive Vice President, North Carolina Department of Community Colleges; and Phail Wynn, Jr., President, Durham Technical Institute.
- Edgar J. Boone, Head, Department of Adult and Community College Education, North Carolina State University, who initially proposed an executive development institute and provided administrative support for the project.
- North Carolina Association of Public Community College Presidents for their endorsement of the proposal and their individual participation in the institute.
- North Carolina Department of Community Colleges and the North Carolina State Board of Community Colleges for the financial support provided.
- Fred W. Manley, Director, Learning Resources, North Carolina Department of Community Colleges, Raleigh, N.C., initial project liaison, and G. Herman Porter, Director, Planning Services, North Carolina Department of Community Colleges, Raleigh, N.C. who served as project liaison.
- Institutions in North Carolina which served as hosts for the institute: Asheville-Buncombe Technical College, Catawba Valley Technical College, Coastal Carolina Community College, Rowan Technical College, Technical College of the Alamance, Wake Technical College, and Wayne Community College.
- Principal resource persons who largely donated their expertise to participate in the institute and provided the necessary review of the final manuscript.
- Mid-Management Task Force for their dedication and persistence in assembling the volume.
- Pamela Grey, Staff Associate, Presidents' Leadership Institute, for her contributions in managing the overall operations of the institute.
- Dave Durham who designed the logo and prepared the accompanying slide tape presentation.
- Alex Beddingfield and Linda Ray for editorial services and preparation of the final manuscript.

- James F. Gollattscheck, Vice President, Information Services, and Mark Winter, Managing Editor, American Association of Community and Junior Colleges, for support in publishing the products of the Institute.

Special notes of thanks are extended to the following people: Richard C. Richardson, Jr. whose thoughts on organizational effectiveness provided a conceptual framework around which to coordinate the recurrent themes of the authors in the manuscript; and to Richard L. Alfred who, while in service as visiting scholar, North Carolina State University, reviewed initial drafts of the manuscript and whose keen insight helped shape the work of the mid-management task force; to Dale Parnell for his leadership and vision for the future of the community college which provides an initial framework of the necessary competencies for a new management style for future community college leaders; and to George B. Vaughan for his initial skepticism, given the enormous number of contributors involved, who wrote after reviewing his chapter: "I honestly believe you are going to pull it off!" If I did not, I bear full responsibility. If we were successful in some small way in contributing to the readers' professional development and to kindling a renewed commitment to our mission of achieving opportunity with excellence, it is due to the contributions of the outstanding professionals who collaborated on this endeavor.

Raleigh, North Carolina
October, 1984

Dale F. Campbell

Introduction

"Many great civilizations in history have collapsed at the height of their achievement because they were unable to analyze their problems, to change direction, and to adjust to new situations which faced them by concerting their wisdom and strength."

Kurt Waldheim

"Action" is the key to effective community college leadership for this decade. George Keller speaks of this action orientation in his book, *Academic Strategy:*

"Leadership is that intangible ability to touch people's nerve endings and cause them to act. It is what a university president must provide, quietly or with fire in his breath, if he is to dignify the enterprise, rouse the disparate faculty and staff into a united drive toward excellence, and defend the work of higher education with cogency and ardor against unknowing or unappreciative assailants."[1]

Viable leadership demands that the problems of higher education be confronted, analyzed and solved by bringing together the right people and resources, and by fostering what Peters and Waterman refer to as "productivity through people—creating in all employees the awareness that their best efforts are essential."[2] The ability to communicate, and the capacity for living by a strong value system are primary to the maintenance of moral leadership viability, and to enhanced institutional productivity through redirection and adaptive change.

The experiences provided by the Presidents' Leadership Institute to help college presidents acquire new management skills and strategies for coping with today's information society have far reaching implications in the areas of strategic planning, governance, human resource development, computer technology and resource management. The challenges of rapid technological developments, a changing economy, increasing competition and a crisis of identity can be met with new motivating competencies and adaptive strategies. The chapters in this volume are organized to share with the reader selected adaptive strategies to enhance community college effectiveness.

In Chapter One, entitled "Strategic Planning," Keller and McClenney maintain that institutional and environmental changes must be confronted on an increasingly accelerated basis by community college educators. These leaders need to accurately interpret these changes, and apply advanced technological tools and management styles to adjust. Bringing about organizational change is primary to strategic planning. The focus on emerging issues which could possibly affect the college several years hence is one of the most discernible of strategic planning's

---

[1]George Keller, *Academic Strategy: The Management Revolution in American Higher Education,* (Baltimore: John Hopkins University Press, 1983).

[2]Thomas J. Peters and Robert H. Waterman, Jr. *In Search of Excellence,* (New York: Harper and Row, 1982).

attributes. For this reason, strategic planning should be considered a part of the decision-making process throughout the institution, and as on-going in nature. Making effective decisions which consider future consequences and orientations is an important part of good management and effective strategic planning. Strategic planning does recognize that the actions of management do, in fact, determine the growth of the institution.

Again, "bringing the right people together" is a vital element of the planning process as leadership draws input from throughout the organization to promote trust and the necessary commitment to be successful in implementing those plans. The nucleus of strategic planning is the common sense of mission. Institutional personnel possess a mutual perception of the college's future, and feel a personal sense of responsibility for achieving its goals because they play a part in the planning process. One of the most powerful motivating tools available to managers and leaders is providing employees with the sense of control over their own destinies and the accompanying meaningful work responsibilities. Resulting shared information of the strategic planning process promotes a sense of trust and common understanding of the institutions's goals and purposes.

Keller emphasizes the importance of effective resource allocation and realistic financial planning in light of the demographic, economic, technological and higher education revolutions on strategic planning. The ability to implement decided strategies may be heavily influenced by state level political controls, governance systems, rigid administrative controls and tax levying capabilities. However, this need not deter college leadership from granting the openness and freedom necessary for creative problem solving within the institution.

Richardson and Vaughan in Chapter Two suggest that designing systems of governance for overall organizational effectiveness as a strategy for "moving their organizations toward the achievement of priorities" is paramount to today's chief executives in producing desired change. Approaching organizations as whole functioning systems when measuring effectiveness assists managers in determining the extent to which the college's established goals are achieved, how positive relationships are continued with external financial resource entities, and the extent to which institutional objectives are supported by those within the institution. Use of participatory management by chief executive officers in formulating policies, setting institutional goals and objectives, and implementing strategies to attain those goals is a requisite part of enabling an institution to function as a unified whole.

Meeting the needs of the client in terms of what are defined as satisfactory outcomes necessitates that the organization change as client demands change for that organization to remain effective. For organizational renewal and adaptation to take place, community colleges must recognize the need for decentralization, and the establishment of new subsystems: they must become "development organizations." Linkages with business and industry, public school systems and four-year colleges require a flexible and effective organizational structure which can be adaptable enough to deal with these external factors.

Well-governed institutions make a free flow of information available to those who are involved in not only the decision-making process, but those who implement "action plans." Internal operations data on facility and equipment meeds, budget amounts, etc. is indispensable. Decentralization of information availability promotes creative and innovative responses to both internal and external environments.

New funding linkages developed and maintained through entrepreneurial vision and business pragmatism mark the strong institutions. Chapter Two also proposes that pricing strategies encompassing "demand-based pricing," "competition-based pricing" and "price discrimination strategy" are capable of producing additional revenues without the negative effects if applied knowledgably. Linkages with industry to promote a cooperative rather than competitive relationship require considerable flexibility to deliver what businesses need in periods of rapid change. However, when entering a relationship with these agencies, the risk of compromising mission must be weighed against the opportunities for achieving effectiveness through these linkages.

Balancing program mix with budgetary constraints must also be considered by governing forces. Flexible management styles, an entrepreneurial orientation to funding sources, and new, more effective organizational structures designed to achieve quality performance in governance are integral factors in the drive to maintain open access, institutional integrity and staff vitality.

The crisis of revenue stabilization throughout the next two decades magnifies the importance of resource allocation on the outcomes or products of educational institutions. Reduced resources and increased competition for those resources, demographic fluctuations, vacillating federal policies, institutional politics, rigid decision-making resulting from increasing state control, aging facilities and the decline in favorable public perceptions are among the foremost problems faced by community college leadership. In Chapter Three on "Leadership and Curricula," the authors recognize the impact of these problems on leadership styles and value systems. Sensitivity to, and support of, the college mission are of paramount importance to administrators in producing the major product of these institutions—learning. Excellence is defined as where the students "are when they leave." Dale Parnell maintains that, "If, in fact, our major product is learning, then everything we do should support learning in the institution." Effective leadership requires the acceptance and understanding of a strong sense of mission and opportunity in higher education.

Human resource development with a focus on computer literacy, management of change, and faculty evaluation and development programs will provide our best answer to the challenge of rapid technology changes over the next decade. Hammons and Hudgins, in the next chapter on "Human Resource Development," discuss the implications of this technological revolution in community college settings which encompass the necessity for constantly accelerating the translation of data into useful information to facilitate decision-making, and access to relevant data by constituent users. Principal to the retrieval of pertinent information, however, is the strategic planning needed to develop these data systems. This requires a "productivity through people" leadership approach to relevant information gathering via composite academic, financial and administrative task forces. Education and personnel training become high priorities as operator qualifications may determine much of the success of the computer system implementation.

Lippitt notes that several trends are emerging in the area of human resource development. More importance is becoming attached to improving performance than on just increasing individual knowledge throughout business, industry and government. There is more training done to deal with situations as opposed to improving individual skills only, and there is more emphasis on evaluation of results. Professional development is considered to be the way that management "gets its job done," and "action learning" is receiving more attention. To ensure that learning is heightened by application, follow-up experiences are being provided for employees. These trends point to higher costs for professional development, but also to more accountability in training and evaluation efforts, and to increased employee productivity resulting from "hands-on" training.[3]

Enhanced institutional responsiveness to fluctuating industrial manpower needs and to the changing supply of available faculty in the high demand areas of the business, engineering and health industries can be implemented through the development of a systematic development program. The three-phased process of evaluation/motivation/development, discussed in Chapter Four, is indicative of an operational and organizational climate which supports learning.

Chapter Five, "Computers and Telecommunications," notes that with the advances of computer technology, consortiums of industry, business, government and educational data bases contribute additional instructional possibilities given the data of various user groups. Instructional policies may change drastically over the next decade as computerized instruction is largely available at any time, and may rely a great deal on the competencies of individual students to advance at different speeds. The authors suggest that there will be funding mechanism modifications, and that credit hour values will also probably change as educational progress will be measured by or linked to competency-oriented evaluation. These innovative policies and data availabilities are other underlying reasons for faculty retraining and professional development, especially through instructional telecommunication. Developing corresponding methods of diagnosing individual learner's needs and learning styles for incorporation into instructional software packages which are learner controlled, and validating instructional packages which are designed and produced outside the institution will require increasing amounts of faculty time, effort and computer expertise.

Because computer systems are becoming increasingly smaller, administrators will have to gain an understanding of interactive office workstations between states and countries via satellite. As it has been predicted that 90% of all computer related costs will be in the areas of software and personnel by the 1990's, the authors maintain that faculty and administrative users will be forced to become even more computer literate to properly take advantage of the flexibility these highly sophisticated software tools offer.

Blong and Keener, in Chapter Six on "Resource Development and Marketing," suggest that community college leadership must learn to fully appreciate the importance of marketing for resource development in order to preserve the opportunity for excellence in its institutions. The uniqueness of the product offered by the community college must be stressed to industry and the community through the college leadership. Accurate environmental and needs assessments, competition analysis, a lucid statement of goals, adequate program development, and pricing/delivery market strategies are all a part of the strategic marketing process to facilitate resource flow, record environmental trends, and promote institutional flexibility. The college president clarifies the value of the community college education product through effective leadership, and recognizes this professional role as a vital one.

The resource development officer also plays a pivotal role in the marketing of the college's product. It is he who imparts the importance of a resource development

---

[3]G. Lippitt, *Organizational Renewal: A Holistic Approach to Organizational Development*, (Englewood Cliffs, N.J.: Prentice Hall, 1982).

program and its program efforts to institutional personnel. It is widely agreed that a successful resource development program must have the support and understanding of college staff members. Presidential guidance and support of this development officer are imperative if the development person is to adequately function as a liaison with grant and gift awarding agencies, or in creatively obtaining other resources.

Marketing efforts must consider more carefully the environment and its clientele over the next decade. Trend analysis and creative financial management which uncover resource possibilities and encourage flexibility are becoming increasingly important. The focus, however, should be on marketing the product of the community college—learning.

The Presidents' Leadership Institute has suggested some viable solutions for college leaders to assist them in coping with these obstacles. Alfred, in "Institutional Impact and Image," suggests that developing a case for "uniqueness" in order to demonstrate to funding sources that the community college can beat the competition in delivering quality educational services is important to the growth and survival of the community college. In order to do this, however, the value of these services must be proven to taxpayers supporting the institution through a socioeconomic impact study or analysis of the college on its community. In addition to facilitating the marketing of student outcomes, this can serve to provide accountability to funding sources by exhibiting cost efficient program delivery. Accountability as a "value for value" medium of exchange instead of just a "dollar for dollar" exchange medium, can be facilitated through the use of these impact studies.

Building stronger relationships with other government and business agencies, expanding revenue sources, making criteria for performance levels clear and systematic, utilizing innovative marketing techniques, conducting institutional research, and grasping opportunities for professional leadership renewal are a few of the solution possibilities to the problems facing the college president.

Creativity and innovation both are needed by the community college today to cope with the changing needs of the clientele. Meeting the needs of the community it serves in terms of satisfactory outcomes necessitates that the organization change as environmental demands change in order to remain effective. Leadership skills and strategies designed to foster success with facilitating learning and to encourage excellence in teaching involve constant updating in order to remain relevant and applicable to situations of sometimes turbulent environmental change, and to preserve moral leadership viability.

A synthesis of the best thoughts of the authors in this volume outlining competencies essential to leaders of the future is referenced in Appendix A. Readers are urged to refer to this self assessment to guide their reading and begin their personal program of leadership development.

Ann Kaneklides, CPA Staff Associate
Department of Adult and Community College Education
North Carolina State University
Mid-Management Task Force
Representative

Chapter 1

STRATEGIC PLANNING: ENSURING INSTITUTIONAL VITALITY

Researcher,
George Keller
Senior Vice President
The Barton-Gillet Company
Baltimore, Maryland

Practitioner,
Byron McClenney
Chancellor
Alamo Community College
San Antonio, Texas

Principal Resource Persons Reviewed in this Chapter

RATIONALE

. . . higher education in the U.S. has entered a revolutionary period, one in which not only the finances and the number of students are changing sharply but also the composition of the entire clientele, kinds of courses and program wanted and schedules for them, the degree of competiveness among colleges, the technology needed on campus, nature of the faculty, and the growing extent of external control and regulations. Colleges and universities clearly need to plan for these—and other—upheavals and to construct a more active, change-oriented management style. The era of laissez faire campus administration is over. The era of academic strategy has begun.

George Keller

If you do not lead your institution through good planning, in effect, you are deciding not to plan; you are deciding not to get the benefits that are available to (your institution); you are deciding not to create the kind of environment that solves problems in a very efficient, straightforward, and effective way.

Byron McClenney

Planning provides a legitimate road map for a rational response to uncertainty and change, facilitates control of organizational operations by collecting information to analyze needs and evaluate its programs and services, and orients the organization to a futuristic leadership stance. Instead of reacting to problem situations only when they arise, the organization attempts to foresee and mitigate potential future problems before they become crises.

Edgar J. Boone

OBJECTIVES

This chapter focuses upon the theoretical and operational aspects of strategic planning in the community college and the external and internal changes which have prompted the introduction of this planning strategy into higher education. The chapter draws upon George Keller's widely acclaimed work on strategic management in America higher education and Byron McClenney's successful incorporation, synthesis and operation of a strategic planning model in the community college setting. This chapter attempts to do the following:

1. define and relate strategic planning approaches to selected aspects of community college mission, governance, finance, curriculum development and educational leadership;
2. identify the major operational steps involved in introducing this planning concept within the organization; and
3. identify and discuss the organizational concerns attendant in introducing the strategic planning approach in the community college setting.

INTRODUCTION

The community college movement once characterized by rapidly increasing enrollment, public and legislative acclaim and a vibrant relevant curriculum has rapidly changed. Higher education in all forms now must confront revolutionizing changes in the environment which have transformed the nature of educational practice. Community college educators must grasp the nature of these changes, gain new skills in identifying and interpreting environmental and institutional changes, and master new technological and management tools if their institutions are to succeed or ultimately survive.

The nature of the community college presidency and that of the senior staff will become closely allied with the corporate marketing strategist as institutions seek to reform the curricula, increase funding, and stabilize student enrollment. Existing planning models will be dysfunctional. Strategic planning, inclusive of all these transformations, now is used to describe the process of educational practice for community college leaders in this new era.

New Realities and New Approaches

The reader of the most recent literature on higher education will discover that higher education, similar to other established social institutions, now is undergoing dramatic changes. Academic observers have attempted to describe the perils and the opportunities that confront educational leaders in the next decade. Like the chorus of a Greek tragedy, critics liken much of higher education to a protagonist blind to his own weaknesses with the powers which rule his world poised to bring it crashing down upon him.

The last two decades have been remarkably successful ones for the community college. But, as more and more observers caution, it is not too difficult to imagine the community college in the role of the protagonist, buoyed with past success, shrugging at the chorus of warnings. Private tradition-based colleges have experienced life-threatening conditions with many institutions failing to exhibit the constitution to survive. Community colleges are no longer exempt from the underlying changes which have threatened these and other institutions. To ignore the example of the private colleges, critics warn, wagers the vitality of other members of higher education. Other observers have gone even further. Richard Alfred suggests that without meaningful action during this period of change community colleges risk becoming a "redundant" organization in American higher education (Alfred 1984).

Sweeping changes now confront community college leaders. Many of the promises of the last decade have become empty as institutions faced reduced funding, legislative incursion into governance and curriculum, and both the number and character of the student population transformed. Each of these quantitative changes has produced what many now characterize as a revolution in higher education practice. Educational leaders are now asked to critically focus on decisions which will affect institutional vitality tomorrow. Leadership has become entrepreneurial. Institutions are reexamining their missions searching for approaches which assure service and security. Old planning approaches are being discarded.

What has emerged is a new form of management or "academic strategy" often termed "strategic planning." It is not, however, "the faddish and imitative attention" given to strategic planning (Jonsen 1984). Rather, it is the deliberate and central focus on effective decision making which characterizes this approach. It is not so much interested in doing things right, but more concerned with doing the right things. "Effectiveness, not efficiency, is the watchword of strategic planning" (Baldridge 1982).

The following chapter presents the observations, analysis and reflections of George Keller and his acclaimed work on identifying the underlying revolutions affecting higher education today and his strategic approaches to management during this period. Secondly, the chapter provides a presentation to strategic planning from the perspective of the community college practitioner. And finally, the authors have attempted to give the reader other critical reflections on strategic planning.

Researcher

Several writers have received public acclaim for their work on societal and technological trends which will affect the nature of American society during the next decade. George Keller has identified four revolutionizing changes within these trends which will profoundly affect the nature and practice of higher education during this period. In his study of management in American higher education, Keller characterizes the tasks of education's chief executives as a four-part responsibility divided among administration, management, governance and leadership.

Much of traditional higher education concentrated on the administration of the campus—ensuring that operational concerns from building maintenance to paycheck disbursement were handled efficiently. Keller argues that the revolutionizing trends within and without higher education have reprioritized executives' tasks. Today, "management" with its focus on future-oriented decisions, has become increasingly important as institutions critically examine their educational program and implement marketing strategies imparted from the boards of American business.

Keller's analysis goes even further than this emphasis upon the marketing focus of management. The revolution within higher education shows a continuing restructuring of governance, with a concomitant shift of campus power from the faculty to the administration. Many campuses have experienced a growing decline in the advocacy of their faculty organizations. Many faculty are reluctant to assume the responsibility for the critical decisions, the strategic decisions on their campus.

Educational leadership, Keller's "poetry of the presidency," assumes a central position as presidents enter the political arena for competition for public funding and inspire institutional staff and faculty as they confront the technological and curriculum changes over the next decade.

All of these tasks, when addressed under Keller's analysis, represent the need for an "academic strategy" for institutional stability and growth. Keller's suggestions to institution leaders correspond to these strategic tasks:

- Leaders are urged to begin realistic financial planning. Educational decisions must be supported by future-directed estimates of financial revenues and expenditures. Leaders are encouraged to begin the use of computer-assisted modeling systems to aid in financial planning.
- Heightened attention must be given to productivity and quality among the faculty, staff and administration.
- All decisions affecting the entire organization must be given more attention, especially those involving faculty appointments and faculty tenure.
- More decisions must be future oriented.

KELLER'S REVOLUTIONS AFFECTING HIGHER EDUCATION

The Demographic Revolution

- The established population centers of the United States have changed in size and makeup and continue to shift, creating a growing census in a few states but a declining census in most others. The sunbelt growth accompanied by a concominant decline in the North Central and Northeast states has considerable impact on the nation's distribution of educational enrollment.
- There will be an enormous and unprecedented drop in the population of traditonal college age students.
- All traditional management practices in higher education have been posited on the assumption of stable or increasing enrollment.
- The decade of 1970-80 experienced the greatest wave of immigration into the United States exceeding the immigration period during the first part of the century. Over 11.5 million immigrants were recorded during this decade and the wave continues at almost 1 million immigrants a year.
- Previous immigration had occured predominantly from Europe and Africa. Over 95% of the immigration is now Asian or Latin American.
- The U.S. is becoming a geriatric society. By 1990, one out of every four citizens will be over the age of 55. There will be an increase in demands for public services for this group placed upon all sources of public revenue.
- This aging phenomena is placing heavier demands upon younger workers who must support these programs. When social security was enacted, seven workers were available to contribute for each beneficiary under the program. Today the ratio has fallen from 4.5 to 1 and the predictions, based upon population data, indicate that this could fall to 3.5 to 1 by the end of the decade.
- The demand for education among this group will be significant. In 1984, over 125,000 senior Americans participated in the elderhostel consortium of

higher education institutions.

The Economic Revolution

- After a century of significant economic growth, the United States economy has entered a period of slower growth. Since 1976 the nation has shifted from an exporting nation to one which continues to register an increasingly unfavorable balance-of-trade.
- The centers of manufacturing are shifting to fast moving aggressive European, Asian and third world countries. Today nearly 30% of all automobiles are manufactured outside of the United States. Over 90% of all consumer electronics are manufactured abroad. Approximately 10 million manufacturing jobs have left the United States due to cheaper foreign labor.
- American exports which once were composed chiefly of manufactured goods are increasingly composed of agricultural products and high technology industrial products.
- The costs of education will increase faster than other sectors of the economy. Education will continue to remain a labor intensive endeavor, not lending itself easily to increases in productivity. With increasing demands on public revenues, the public and funding sources will demand cost reductions and increased productivity resulting in future political concerns for educational leaders.

The Technological Revolution

- The surge of new technology is continuing and gaining.
- Computers and new telecommunications represent the most important development in information processing since the printing press.
- The new computer and communications technology is transforming the traditional art of teaching and the nature of educational delivery. In 1984, Japan will introduce a "broadcast" university which utilizes public television to deliver a range of collegiate courses to the Japanese public. The technology is in place today to create an all American University in which the most distinguished faculty in all fields would reside and prepare instructional programs for satellite transmission across the nation.
- The traditional emphasis given to mechanical engineering and metallurgy is rapidly being replaced with an increased emphasis to electronic engineering and materials science.

The Revolution in Higher Education

- Postsecondary education, which once was characterized as a post high school experience, is now rapidly being replaced with the recognition that colleges and universities are similar to the nation's great public libraries in which adults return throughout their personal and professional lives to gain new knowledge and insight.
- This changing characterization is reflected in the changing student profiles which now show that over 36% of the nation's enrollment in higher education is composed of the nontraditional student. Over 40% of the students attend part-time.
- The faculty composition is shifting from the traditional lifetime tenure ap-

pointment track to newer models allowing faculty members the opportunity for consulting. Today over one-third of the nation's faculty are considered part-time.

- United States higher education has become increasingly a United Nation's of citizenships. In the engineering sciences, almost one of every three Phd's granted is awarded to a foreign student.
- Higher education is having difficulty adapting to the community college curriculum. The traditional curriculum was designed to introduce students to general principles and knowledge and to progress to specialized study. Today students enter many instituions with specialized coursework from the community college seeking a more general understanding of the principles supporting the technology.
- Higher education's monopoly on adult education has been relinquished to a growing plethora of institutions and agencies which have a vested interest in adult development. Today one out of very six museums offers college-level courses. Private business spends over $14 billion annually on employee development. Several corporations have actually begun the operation of company colleges awarding undergraduate or graduate degrees. The armed services continue to provide the bulk of much of the nation's technical training. Roughly 50% of the electronic technicians now serving the private sector received their training in the military.

Practitioner

Byron McClenney, as a community college president with experience in three state systems of education and governance, developed and utilized a strategic planning model which was successfully implemented in a broad range of institutions. McClenney defines strategic planning as a "stream of wise decision making."Similar to Keller's characterization, it is a focus on decision making which distinguishes this planning approach from its predecessors.

McClenney has found that strategic planning, when properly introduced in the community college, can achieve a series of positive institutional outcomes including:

- Improved goal orientation: strategic planning focuses the institution's faculty and staff toward a common or collective vision of the institution's future and their common destiny.
- Higher expectations: the planning process instills a sense of mutual expectation and high standards for performance as individuals gain new insights into their personal contribution and its relationship to organization goals.
- Meaningful work: the renewed sense of organizational purpose and objectives and the importance of individual contribution to this purpose provides meaning to employee work responsibilities and improves motivation.
- Collaborative relationships: the collaborative nature of the planning process ensures that cooperative problem solving becomes an internal mode of operation for the college staff and faculty freeing the chief executive and senior staff from operational concerns.
- Integration of resources: strategic planning directly ties the budgeting process with decisions made in the educational and support divisions of the college. This emphasis on effective resource allocation promotes efficiency and eliminates redundancy of functions. Institutions "get more done with less."

- Coping with realities: institutions which use the strategic planning model are constantly forced to examine the changing nature of their external environment and to seek to adapt the institution to these changes. This market scanning promotes a realistic sense of the institution's position in the community and higher education.
- Promotes trust: the collaborative nature of the planning process and the mutual understanding of the institution's purpose and goals helps achieve a desired level of trust within the faculty and staff. All college employees are confronted with the realization that changes in programs or services require a reallocation of resources and that these resources are finite. Many of the mysteries of administrative action and their apparent arbitrary nature can be understood in light of shared information.

McClenney argues that strategic planning is a straightforward process that can be successful with proper attention given to a series of planning essentials which he has observed in his professional practice. McClenney recommends that strategic planning should be viewed as an integral function of management that greatly impacts on the welfare of the institution and its community. Implicit in this acknowledgement is the view of the community college president as the chief planner and spokesman for the planning effort if planning is to be effective.

All planning efforts must be accompanied by the commitment of institutional leaders if planning is to be successful. McClenney warns that the planning process should not begin until institutional leaders are committed.

Strategic planning must be viewed as an ongoing process which involves the internal and external assessment of the institution's programs and services. Planning involves the continuous fine tuning of the available data into useful information available to those involved in the planning program. Institutions should resist the false assumption that planning cannot begin until adequate information is available. For many institutional problems, full information will not be available regardless of the time and effort expended on institutional research. Therefore, recognizing the credibility of people translating data into useful information and making use of available data is crucial.

All strategic planning efforts center upon an institution's clear sense of mission. Institutional leaders must communicate strongly that this mission and its central focus guides the entire planning program. Similarly, all planning must be predicated upon an explicit set of planning assumptions and organizational goals. These assumptions should be continuously reevaluated to ensure that organizational goals remain both relevant and realistic.

The entire planning effort should be guided by a "plan for planning." This plan should provide all institutional members a statement on both the format and the schedule to be used for the planning program. McClenney further suggests that planning should be compacted in an intense compressed time period rather than allowing it to malinger over several months.

Strategic planning is concerned with effecting organizational change, not in developing an intricate management system. The process should be simple and workable, and should avoid any tendency to become a paper mill.

The planning horizon should always extend beyond the next year. The distinguishing characteristic of strategic planning is its focus on critical issues and a stream of wise decision-making which could affect the organization whether those issues become significant within three, seven or ten years.

The entire planning process should be incorporated into the mainstream of institutional decisionmaking. Institutional leaders should insist that operational decisions conform to the overall institutional plan. The link between planning and decision-making should be consistent.

All institutional budgeting should become an outgowth of the planning process. Planning should be viewed as a prerequisite for the allocation or reallocation of resources.

Institutional leaders should recognize that the value of strategic planning lies in the process of planning.

McClenney's experience also has revealed that many of the organizational barriers to strategic planning are common to a wide series of institutions. Similar to his list of planning essentials presented previously, McClenney also has provided a list of many of the most prevalent barriers to planning in the community college setting:

- Futility: Many faculty and staff members are reluctant to attempt planning because the institution has ignored past planning efforts.
- Time: Many managers occupy themselves with operational and lower order administrative tasks.
- Commitment: Many individuals are uncommitted to planning or any additional responsibilities placed upon them.
- Complexity: Planning involves a complexity of interrelated variables which are difficult to isolate and arrange relative to one another.
- Resistance to Change: Planning often leads to organizational changes which are resisted by many individuals. These individuals resist planning as a precursor to such undetermined changes.
- Resources: Many institutions fail to plan under the assumption that the process involves the allocation of resources which are not available to the institution.
- Self-interest: Similar to the resistance to change, many institutions refrain from planning due to the vested self-interests of many institutional officers.
- Mission: Institutions must have a clear sense of mission before planning can begin. The lack of a clear mission inhibits planning.
- External resistance: Many institutions face opposition to changes in mission or programs from their publics with vested interest in the institution's program.
- Activity: Institutions do not tend to develop an annual cycle of activity to update the strategic plan, develop the operational plan, and allocate or reallocate resources resulting in confusion and disorganization.
- Involvement: *All* levels of the institution's organization are not involved in developing achievements and results of the current year, desired outcome for next year and projections for the second year of the cycle causing hostility and ultimately disinterest among staff.

Strategic Planning, the Organization and Organization Development

Drucker (1980) in *Managing in Turbulent Times*, observed that managers of all organizations face one unifying challenge. "The one certainty about the times ahead, the times in which managers will have to work and to perform, is that they will be turbulent times. And in turbulent times, the first task of management is to make sure of the institution's capacity for survival, to make sure of its structural strength and soundness, of its capacity to survive a blow, to adapt to sudden change, and avail itself of new opportunities."

Kim Cameron distinguishes between organization adaptation and organization development efforts of institutions as they seek Drucker's desired internal capacity and structural strength. "Organizational adaptation refers to modifications and alterations in the organization or its components in order to adjust to changes in the external environment. Its purpose is to restore equilibrium to an imbalanced condition. Adaptation generally refers to a process, not an event, whereby changes are instituted in organizations. Adaptation does not necessarily imply reactivity on the part of an organization . . . because proactive or anticipatory adaptation is possible as well. But the emphasis is definitely on responding to some discontinuity or lack of fit that arises between the organization and its environment" (Cameron 1984). Organization development focuses upon changes resulting from internal factors of the organization. (Both are important for the successful use of strategic planning.)

Organizational charts have undergone considerable change in the past years at institutions adapted to the "lack-of-fit" between the external and the internal factors. Community colleges adapted to the reduced enrollment and funding with the creation of positions in public information, marketing and resource development. But the difficulty is in envisioning the successful incorporation of these staff functions into the organization without an institution's use of organization development strategies to reduce contervailing forces to internal change and strengthen faculty and staff acceptance of the legitimacy of these new functions.

In her study of successful strategic management practices in small private colleges, Chaffee found that institutions which recognized the importance of guiding and interpreting organizational change to the college community (practicing organization development) were more resilient to environmental threats facing these institutions than those which merely adapted to changes in market demands (practiced organization adaptation) (Chaffee 1984). McClenney's approach to strategic planning emphasizes the importance of organizational involvement without abdicating Keller's task of "management" and "leadership."

Other researchers have drawn attention to the intimate relationship between many strategic planning models and approaches to organizational development. Walter Hunter (1983) has described a "radical intervention" planning model which, similar to McClenney's approach, casts strategic planning in an organizational intensive framework.

> In the truest sense the rational intervention method is a "quality circle" approach. It is based on the premise that good people will adjust. Redirect. Change in a democratic way when presented with information which is critical to their continued existence within the total institution.

Hunter describes the approach as proceeding in seven stages overlapping with many of those used by McClenney:

1. There is an awareness of the problem.
2. Relevant information is assimilated.
3. The problem is fully defined.
4. Alternate solutions are considered.
5. An alternate is selected.
6. The alternate is fully refined in a safe environment.
7. The change is adopted.

The similarity to McClenney's approach is not coincidental. Strategic planning in its focus to change redirects organization goals and inputs through changes in human resources. Chaffee's study provides empirical evidence which confirms the importance of both organizational adaptation and organizational development in successful strategic planning.

Accepting Institutional Boundaries

The traditional planning models utilized by higher education over the past decades focused upon the use of resources in meaningful cost-effective ways. Planning was apolitical with planning models drawing extensively upon business principles grounded in economics. Institutional leaders were internally focused. Strategic planning, as characterized by Keller and McClenney, recognizes the political environment as the fundamental arena where decisions regarding governance, finance and curriculum are formulated. Parnell underscores the significance of this new orientation:

> A word we tend to shy away from but which is a concern as an external factor is the word "politics." Too many of our people tend to think politics is a dirty business and we are not going to be involved in it. I want to tell you that every day I walk into my office I am in politics. Everyday a president walks into his office he is involved in politics. There is nothing more fierce than politics on a college campus.

Strategic planning focuses upon the ability of an institution to adopt locally initiated strategies that are consistent with local needs and regional or state level priorities. Each individual institution, however, possesses widely varying opportunities for change and adaptation which have been developed and nurtured within the political environment. Increasing amounts of state governance and state fiscal dependence, for instance, represent decreasing opportunities for institutional action. In general, community colleges differ in their ability to invoke new strategies for renewal in three areas.

Community colleges are now established within two principal patterns of control: (1) states in which two year colleges are fully controlled by the state, and (2) states where two year colleges are controlled by both local communities and the state. Few institutions can be characterized as fully independent of state control. In 1984, 40 states provided for some type of board at the state level with varying degrees of control as the principal governing body for their community colleges (Campbell 1984). Coordinated state systems of community colleges and state systems of higher education regulate institution's curriculum programs. The community college movement that once was characterized as 'the most adaptive system of education' has in many states become fully incorporated into a bureaucracy which parallels that of a regulated public utility. Educational leaders must recognize that strategic plans should address both the changes which can be introduced within the existing system of governance and seek the necessary local autonomy to ensure the institution's ability to adapt to local needs.

Dale Parnell (1984), in describing the dominant factors affecting community colleges in the future, challenged community colleges to avoid unnecessary rigidity in administrative control.

> I hope that community colleges never lose their flexibility: that's been the hallmark of the growth of the community college movement; but I am afraid that I see some of the hardening of the arteries

setting in. We are making a few more rules, the states are making a few more rules, and the federal government is making a few more rules. There was a report put out on higher education, I believe Milton Eisenhower was the editor of it, back in the late 50's. I remember the title of it, "Efficiency in Freedom." There is some efficiency in allowing local control and in allowing some freedom for people to move . . . .

Perhaps even greater disparity exists in community college finance. Some states allow institutions or districts to levy taxes for capital and operational support. Other states provide no opportunity for institutional assessment instead providing the institution with funds under a state established enrollment driven formula. Again leaders must work within established systems of finance but actively campaign for changes in finance and funding formulas which circumscribe institution's abilities to meet student demands and introduce new programs and services which meet the emerging community needs identified through needs assessment and analysis.

In their award winning book, *In Search of Excellence*, Peters and Waterman (1982) characterize America's best run businesses as loose-tight organizations, organizations which adhere tightly to a central marketing strategy or business philosophy while retaining the looseness needed to promote creativity and responsiveness to customers and employees. Community college leaders should not utilize strategic plans to focus upon policies, formulas or systems of governance which fail to promote institutional vitality.

IMPLICATIONS

New Challenges for Strategic Planning

The management literature is replete with examples of management systems which were introduced as the culmination of the management sciences. Much of the early literature on management-by-objectives, program planning and budgeting systems, and zero-based budgeting endorsed these models as tools which would achieve the zenith of organizational vitality and effectiveness. Many of these systems continue to serve organizations; however, their initial fascination has faded.

Strategic planning, especially as presented by Keller and McClenney, has not been presented as an algorithm to solve the problems facing community college leaders. It is instead the rational realization that what management does or does not do affects the growth and survival of an organization. But, as leaders accept and begin the task of strategic management within the community college, meaningful challenges emerge which must be acknowledged and successfully incorporated into approaches to community college planning.

Challenges to Mission

As community college leaders use strategic planning to analyze their individual missions and seek new student markets, the commitment to open access and educational opportunity can be undermined. Keller's "active, entrepreneurial shaping of an organization's or institution's future life . . ." does not license an institution to abandon its public charter and trusts. Declining financial aid resources and the growing cost of remedial instruction might suggest that an institution develop and market programs and services to students with ability to pay. The college leaders could raise admission standards thereby reducing the costs of remediation. Alternatively, the college could seek new sources of financial aid and develop a new cost-effective delivery system for remedial instruction.

Both Keller and McClenney emphasize that strategic planning offers only a framework for decision making which focuses relevant information on our choices. Within this framework, community college leaders must seek strategies which ensure institutional vitality without abandoning the commitment to the publics the institutions were chartered to serve.

Challenges to Organization Development

Keller and McClenney both emphasize the involvement of all organizational levels in the strategic planning process. McClenney's model, with it seven institutional outcomes, provides for organization renewal and development as strategic planning is introduced as an ongoing process involving all levels of the community college. Keller, writing from his observations of higher education at all levels, notes that political power has "shifted from the faculty to the campus leaders . . . (and that) the choice has passed to the administrators to make the new, hard decisions."

Indeed, strategic planning has moved to the forefront of the staff development field as educational leaders deal with retrenchment and critically analyze their programs and services. Many observers have noted that faculty have shown a great reluctance to make the "new, hard decisions." The effective educational leader must bridge the chasm between these two organizational realities. Leaders must draw upon all levels of the organization in the planning process if a desirable climate of trust and vitality is maintained. However, leaders must recognize that many midlevel managers and faculty cannot shoulder the responsibility to abolish the programs staffed by their colleagues. Even greater conflicts are apparent when the positions of collective bargaining faculty groups counter those of the administration.

Keller describes the efforts of Princeton, Ohio University, Temple and Northwestern as they seek to bridge the seemingly competing needs of organizational involvement and decisive strategic planning. In this process new forms of governance in higher education have often emerged. The creation and effective use of these new organizational structures may represent the principal challenge to community college leaders as they introduce strategic planning within their institutions.

CONCLUSION

This chapter has briefly discussed the use of strategic planning as a new conceptual model to guide community college leaders in addressing the complex challenges of the next decades. There is no attempt here to present this approach as the last management panacea for higher education. Strategic planning does, however, provide a structured approach to decision making which requires institutions to project the long term consequences of operational decisions that have frequently gone unexamined.

As institutions implement strategic responses, new challenges to institutional missions, governance and finance will emerge. Educational leaders must recognize that many planning responses risk the abandonment of the founding mission of the community college movement. Creative leaders are needed to bridge the community college's tradition of access and opportunity with the financial and technological realities colleges now face.

Reviewers for this Chapter

William J. Starling
Dean of Administrative Services
Sampson Technical College
Clinton, North Carolina

John M. Duncan
Engineering and Vocational Division
    Counselor
Fayetteville Technical Institute
Fayetteville, North Carolina

REFERENCES

Alfred, R. L. "Paradox for Community Colleges: Education in the '80's." *Community College Review* 12, no. 1 (Summer 1984): 2-6.

Baldridge, J. V., and P. H. Okimi. "Strategic Planning in Higher Education: New Tool or Old Gimmick?" *American Association for Higher Education Bulletin* 35, no. 2 (October 1982): 6, 15-18.

Boone, E. J. *Developing Programs in Adult Education.* Englewood Cliffs, N.J.: Prentice Hall, 1984.

Cameron, K. S. "Strategic Responses to Conditions of Decline: Higher Education and the Private Sector." *Journal of Higher Education* 54, no. 4 (July/August 1983): 359-80.

_____. "Organizational Adaptation and Higher Education." *Journal of Higher Education* 55, no. 2 (March/April 1984): 122-44.

Campbell, D. F. "Patterns of Control for Public Community Colleges." Department of Adult and Community College Education, North Carolina State University, 1984.

Chaffee, E. E. "Turnaround Management Strategies: The Adaptive Model and the Constructive Model." National Center for Higher Education Management Systems, Boulder, Colorado: March 1983.

_____. "Successful Strategic Management in Small Private Colleges." *Journal of Higher Education* 55, no. 2 (March/April 1984): 212-41.

Drucker, P. F. *Managing in Turbulent Times.* New York, N.Y.: Harper and Row, 1980.

Hunter, W. "The Future of Postsecondary Education: How Is P. S. Education Being Shaped?" Paper presented to Missouri Community Junior Colleges, Tantara, Lake of the Ozarks, October 1983.

Jonsen, R. "Small Colleges Cope with the Eighties: Sharp Eye on the Horizon, Strong Hand on the Tiller." *Journal of Higher Education* 55, no. 2 (March/April 1984): 171-83.

Keller, G. *Academic Strategy: The Management Revolution in American Higher Education.* Baltimore: The Johns Hopkins University Press, 1983a.

_____. "Strategic Planning - Implications for Leadership." Paper presented at the Presidents' Leadership Institute, Wake Technical College, Raleigh, North Carolina, October 1983b.

McClenney, B. *Management for Productivity.* Washington, D.C.: AMerican Association of Community and Junior Colleges, 1980.

_____. "Organizational Development: A President's View." In *Organization Development Change Strategies.* New Directions for Community Colleges, no. 37. San Francisco: Jossey-Bass, 1982.

_____.*Strategic Planning - Implications for Leadership.* Paper presented at the Presidents' Leadership Institute, Wake Technical College, Raleigh, North Carolina, October 1983.

Parnell, D. "Opportunity with Excellence: Vision of the Future." Interview by Dale F. Campbell and Robert M. Stivender, 13 June 1984. Tape recording, American Association of Community and Junior Colleges, Washington, D.C.

Chapter 2

GOVERNANCE:
STRUCTURE, STYLE AND FINANCE

Researcher,
Richard C. Richardson, Jr.
Professor of Higher Education
Arizona State University
Tempe, Arizona

Practitioner,
George B. Vaughan
President
Piedmont Virginia Community
    College
Charlottesville, Virginia

Principal Resource Persons Reviewed in this Chapter

RATIONALE

What we really need to concern ourselves with is organizational effectiveness. After all, our national slogan is "opportunity with excellence" and this implies attention to how well we are doing whatever we have set out to do. Most discussions I have heard among presidents avoid the effectiveness question. Partly, this follows from our inability to define what we mean by effectiveness or excellence; but also present is an element of concern. If we do assess our effectiveness and discover that it is less than it should be, how will we cope with this finding? People sometimes avoid physical examinations for the same reason.

Richard C. Richardson, Jr.

The community college must be willing to be flexible and seek solutions to old and new problems without abandoning those tenets of its philosophy that have made it valuable to American society.

George B. Vaughan

At a gut level, all of us know that much more goes into the process of keeping a large organization vital and responsive than the policy statements, new strategies, plans, budgets and organization charts can possibly depict. But all too often we behave as though we don't know it. If we want change, we fiddle with the strategy or we change the structure. Perhaps the time has come to change our ways.

Thomas J. Peters and
Robert H. Waterman

OBJECTIVES

By the end of this chapter the reader should be able to:

1. Understand the environmental characteristics that influence organizational effectiveness in community colleges.
2. Discuss some recognized models of organizational effectiveness and approaches to using them for evaluating outcomes in community colleges.
3. Identify some of the administrative practices currently in use to promote organizational effectiveness.
4. Distinguish between those community college goals and objectives which may be successfully altered and those that are altered at the risk of distorting the true community college mission.

INTRODUCTION

Organizational Effectiveness

Finance and governance should be studied as means to an end rather than as ends in themselves or even as discrete topics. Researchers of organizational development emphasize that to be effective in producing desired change, managers must approach their organizations as functioning systems. Their point is that within a system, changes in any element affect all of the other elements, and the impact of these changes must be taken into account so that changes are additive rather than contradictory. CEOs are not fascinated with finance and governance as topics deserving of study in their own right (which of course they are), but rather as strategies for moving their organizations toward the achievement of priorities. Richard C. Richardson, Jr., Professor and Chairman of the Department of Higher and Adult Education at Arizona State University used these words to introduce his presentation to the North Carolina Community Colleges Presidents Leadership Institute.

Richardson's model, "Managing for Organizational Effectiveness," provides an excellent framework for a review of his thinking on the subject. (See Figure 1). Commenting on the exhibit, Richardson says, "The model includes three distinct clusters of variables. The first involving organizational characteristics, some of which can be changed by managers while others are largely outside organizational influence. It is on these characteristics that most discussions I have heard among presidents focus. Like good hypochondriacs, we derive considerable satisfaction and a certain amount of relief by comparing symptoms and discovering that ours are no worse than anyone else's."

The organizational characteristics section of the effectiveness model clearly delineates those environmental characteristics over which practitioners exercise little or no direct control. These can, however, be influenced (as found later in this discussion) and therefore usually command a good deal of attention from top line administrators. On the other hand, the administrative characteristics listed in the model are elements over which control can be directly maintained.

Most community college leaders have no doubt felt the frustration of constraining funding formulas or system-wide goals and objectives that seem inappropriate to meet local needs. "If only we had a better quality student! You had better be gald you don't have to work with the faculty at our institution! Why doesn't the public appreciate the urgency of what we are trying to do out here!" These and similar comments might be heard on any community college campus from California to

Managing for Organizational Effectiveness

ORGANIZATIONAL CHARACTERISTICS	MANAGEMENT PRACTICES	OBSERVABLE OUTCOMES
Environmental a. Fiscal Constraints Including Methods of Funding b. Mission Definition (state) c. Student Demographics (age, preparation, full-time/part-time, educational objectives) d. Faculty Characteristics (tenure, field of preparation, recency of training) e. Public Priorities (prisons, economic development)	*To Alter Environment* a. Legislative Activity b. Public Information Program c. Community Service Management Roles: liaison, monitor, spokesman, negotiator — after Mintzberg 1973.	*Organizational Effectiveness* Relationships with external agencies on which college depends for resources *Organizational Effectiveness* Institutional climate including attitudes and level of support from faculty, staff and students
Administrative a. Priorities (access/achievement, efficiency/effectiveness) b. Management Roles c. Decision Processes d. Communication e. Structure	*To Manage the Organization* a. Strategic Planning and Marketing (includes resource allocation, student recruiting) b. Reorganization and Staffing (Colleges without Walls, part-time faculty) c. Participation in Decision Making (includes governance) d. Staff Development (management by objectives, training session) e. Directionality and Openness of Communication f. Evaluation (accountability, program review, institutional research on outcomes) Management Roles: leader, monitor, disseminator, entrepreneur, disturbance handler, resource allocator	*Organizational Effectiveness* Goal Achievement

(Richardson 1983)

Figure 1

the Carolinas. While the complaints may be to no avail, there are appropriate strategies which can successfully impact these environmental characteristics. Even where they cannot be altered, these characteristics must be understood since they provide the context within which community colleges function.

It is less fashionable, but just as important, to talk about those administrative characteristics of priority setting, management role definition, decision-making processes, communication channels and organizational structure. Clearly, these elements are controllable and more directly addressed than the environmental ones.

Before looking at the management practices that attempt to influence and control the organizational characteristics that Richardson identifies, it is helpful to have some gauge of the effectiveness of those practices. Professor Richardson comments, "If we really want to make our organizations more effective, and the decade of the 80's has already emerged as an era concerned with quality, then we must find out how well we are currently doing or we will have no basis for deciding what changes, if any, are necessary."

Richardson continues, "Excellence is one extreme on a scale on which we measure effectiveness." He goes on to outline three tracks along which organizational effectiveness runs in the pursuit of excellence. These tracks measure:

- The extent to which the college's established goals are achieved.
- The extent to which positive relationships are maintained with the external entities which the college depends on for resources.
- The extent to which positive relationships within the institution prompt people to support the objectives of the institution.

As was the case with the organizational characteristics, the three definitions of organizational effectiveness feature both internal and external elements. Also present is a sense of a mix of the controllable and the uncontrollable. Again, the implication is prudence dictates aggressiveness in attending to the controllable and less paralysis from fears about the uncontrollable.

What happens when one definition of effectiveness conflicts with another? Richardson cites an example of an institution whose administration felt the need for a new set of institutional priorities that conflicted with the faculty-perceived accepted norms of operation. Specifically, the administration took steps to establish a "college without walls," a strong continuing education outreach program involving the hiring of part-time faculty from the community. There was resistance from the old guard college-transfer oriented faculty on grounds of educational principle. Furthermore, the change hit the pocketbook of faculty members when the continuing education classes they taught for extra income moved off campus.

Here is a clear illustration of a conflict between the organizational effectiveness measurement of goal achievement and the maintenance of an internal climate supportive of the institution's objectives. Other examples can readily come to mind.—A much needed budget request for a faculty pay raise is proposed to a funding authority that has taken a stand against new taxes. Or, there is a push for improved funding for the college transfer program in a climate where the college's primary mission is job training. Amid all these obvious conflicts, Richardson is quick to point out that "to the extent that you pursue one form of effectiveness, that may mitigate against your ability to achieve another form of effectiveness."

When it comes to management style, Richardson relies heavily upon the work of Henry Mintzberg on managerial roles. "It is Mintzberg's (1973) contention that administrators influence the organizations they lead through the relative emphasis they place on each of ten managerial roles. (See Appendix B). An administrator's preference for a particular role influences choice of strategies and the approach taken to implementation. For example, Mintzberg's research suggests that managers in general show preference for brevity and interruption in their work. Thus, a tendency toward superficiality becomes a prime occupational hazard for the manager. This preference in turn relates to the role of disturbance handler which many managers enjoy. (In fact, some have been suspected of creating disturbances so that they can have the satisfaction of dealing with them)."Noting the roles that Richardson identifies as appropriate for community college leaders in their efforts to alter and internally manage the institution's environment is interesting and worthwhile.

The principle of adjusting or radically changing strategies over time is an accepted one. Richardson points out that likewise, altering management styles is necessary. Returning to the example of conflict between forms of effectiveness, the administration initially acted very autocratically in establishing the "college without walls." Sensing the internal discontent, the administration involved the faculty in a planning process indicative of a very democratic style. By this adaptation of management styles, the administration quickly placed its priorities and moved to regain the internal support needed to assure the institution's continued progress.

Richardson makes reference to the work of Fredrick Redin whose managerial grid introduces an effectiveness dimension. Redin's idea is that managers should be aware of the prevalent management style within their institution and be prepared to adjust it when inhibiting overall organizational effectiveness. The relative importance of knowing one's own management style and the management tools available becomes clear. This mix of style and strategy working to create a favorable external environment, a supportive climate within the institution, and a well-conceived set of goals will produce excellence in our community colleges.

Mission

While few would dispute the need to be effective in the external environment or within the institution, not all community college practitioners are as willing as Richardson appears to be to compromise the traditional goals of community colleges.

One such individual is George B. Vaughan, President of Piedmont Virginia Community College. He admits that the community college is facing a crossroads where re-examination of its priorities, its resources and its mission are in order. However, Vaughan cautions against "abandoning those tenets of its philosophy that have made it valuable to American society."

As Vaughan (1983) stated, today's managers, in order to be more effective as leaders, need to first clarify the mission of the community college. He says the mission is difficult to articulate for several reasons: the mission is constantly changing and stays in a "constant state of flux"; each community college has its own mission which makes it different in certain aspects from the national mission; and the change in leadership at the national level has taken the colleges in a different direction. The last reason refers to the change in the presidency of the American Association of Community and Junior Colleges from Edmund Gleazer to Dale Parnell. Gleazer was a philosophical leader who envisioned the community college as a "student-centered, community-based, performance-oriented people's college." Parnell, on the other hand, is a pragmatist and has placed the emphasis on establishing strong linkages with business and industry to improve training and retraining programs.

Community colleges, according to Vaughan, may be at a watershed. The mission may or may not be changing; but as Cohen (1982) says, if it is not, at least the emphasis is shifting. Vaughan says that community college leaders need to find a broad perspective around which they can rally to revitalize the mission, and he suggests that maintaining institutional integrity may be that needed perspective. He lists six trends which he feels are now threatening institutional integrity:

1. *The Quality Revolution.* An emphasis on quality tends to result in the exclusion of that segment of society which has depended on the community college as its only source for educational improvement. If institutional integrity is to be maintained, quality must be defined only in terms that are compatible with the mission of the college.
2. *Partnership with Business and Industry.* As closer linkages are established with business and industry, college leaders must not allow business and industry to dictate educational policy and decision making.
3. *Loss of Comprehensiveness.* Community colleges must resist the temptation to offer only those courses which show a profit. Students must have a choice of programs in order for the institution to maintain its integrity.
4. *Loss of Funding for Community Service.* With shrinking funds from legislators to fund recreational and personal interest courses, leaders must determine if the community services component needs to be dropped from the mission. If not, supplemental funding sources need to be found.
5. *Increasing Costs to Students.* The last few years have seen an increase in tuition and a corresponding decrease in available financial aid. This most directly affects that socio-economic component of society which only the community colleges have been able to adequately serve. Leaders must assure that this part of the mission of the community college does not have to be dropped.
6. *Abrogation of Decision-Making Powers.* Community college leaders have not been able to make the distinction between decisions that should be made by them and those that should be made by lawmakers and other parties. As a result, managers are letting other people make their decisions for them. Managers need to articulate their role so that the lines of authority are clear for all parties involved.

Vaughan (1984) says that leaders must be sensitive to all of these threats, any of which would mean the end of the most important contribution of the community colleges—open access. The case for open access, he says, is simple: this country was founded on the belief that all people have the right, and should have the opportunity, to achieve the full limits of their abilities.

America is changing and education must change to keep up. Vaughan (1984) mentions three factors of which managers need to be aware which could easily move the community colleges in a new direction: (1) declining numbers of high school students; (2) the change in national leadership (which was previously mentioned); and (3) an evolving economy. He says that community colleges must remain flexible and must seek answers to old and new problems while maintaining those tenets of their philosophy which have made them so successful.

Vaughan says that the community college has four areas of concern which managers must now deal with.

1. *Maintaining Open Access.* The community college represents the only chance millions of Americans have to further their education beyond high school. But as many community college programs become more complex in nature, the concept of open access is changing and the college is becoming desirable to a different kind of student.

   Several factors are threatening to restrict open access as it is recognized today, including the public challenge to offering high school level courses at the post-secondary level at the public's expense. Other factors which are causing managers to reconsider open access are greater demands for accountability; fewer tax dollars for the support of community service functions and the social side of education; a decline in the support of legislators; the popularity of "high-tech" programs; and a renewed interest in quality. The "quality revolution," Vaughan fears, will be misinterpreted by community colleges and may be used to exclude less-qualified applicants who are members of lower socio-economic levels or minorities. Quality must be considered, but in light of the mission of the community college. He says to automatically accept the better qualified student is to reject the commitment to open access.

2. *Maintaining a Comprehensive Program.* Vaughan sees a comprehensive program as a means for achieving the end, which is open access. There are threats to the comprehensiveness issue. Remedial courses have already been mentioned as an issue with the legislature. Transfer programs have suffered as a result of the emphasis put on technical education. Community service programs have been attacked all across the country. Even vocational programs and student services have been cut back as the more glamorous high-tech programs are expanded. The community college has been the only comprehensive post-secondary institution in the past, but today the picture is changing. Many community colleges are drastically cutting back or dropping various programs altogether.

3. *Institutional Integrity.* The threat to institutional integrity stems from the commitment the community college has to its community. The colleges have established relationships with business, industry and other agencies which have been beneficial to all parties. Vaughan warns managers, however, that these relationships can become dangerous if not monitored carefully. He says that compromise is the answer to such relationships. He thinks representatives from industry, for example, *should* be involved in faculty selection and assessment of performance. He says partnerships with other agencies should become an integral part of the total operation of the college. In this way a system of checks and balances is formed through the faculty, staff, administration and governing board, which will help maintain institution integrity while fulfilling its objective that calls for cooperation between outside agencies.

4. *Keeping Faculty and Staff Vital.* Vaughan offers no answers for this concern, but he does describe how conditions have changed over the years and now are working against faculty and administrative vitality. By 1992 over 52% of all college faculty members will be over 55 years old. Community colleges have less courses to be taught than the four-year institutions. Therefore, a faculty member will be called on to teach the same course year after year. These people are certainly subject to burnout unless something can be found to remedy the situation. As growth has slowed, so has the demand for new

faculty and administrators. Mobility has slowed to a crawl. Faculty just do not have the opportunity to move from job to job as they once did. As Vaughan says, "Innovation is a rarely heard word on most community college campuses today; faculty members are playing it safe for reasons of limited funds, public image and job security."

Vaughan says that the community college can survive this crisis and become even stronger if managers can learn to build upon its strengths and continue to serve the needs of society in an efficient and effective way.

Governance Relationships

If Richardson is accurate in defining the three forms of effectiveness, and if Vaughan's thinking on the need to preserve the basic tenets of the community college mission is acceptable, this establishes a somewhat different twist in the pursuit of excellence. This concept is best illustrated visually.

Envision Richardson's three forms of effectiveness as individual scales along which effectiveness runs toward the extreme of excellence. Now, imagine that the three tracks converge at the point of excellence. In graphic form the image will appear as Figure 2. This model assumes, as Vaughan argues, that the central community college mission (goals) should not be subjected to the give and take that Richardson argues must take place between the forms of excellence. Given this assumption, the achievement of excellence becomes a function of those relationships that comprise the institution's external and internal environment.

Organizational Effectiveness Model

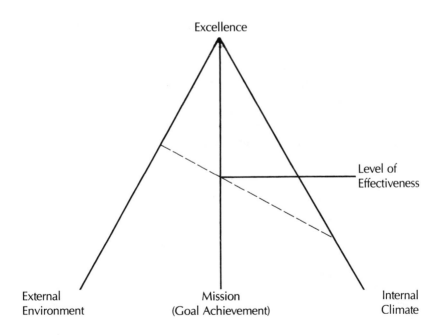

Figure 2

Using the model diagram, select a point on the external environment continuum that might represent an institution's relationship with its external environment (prospective students, business and industry, funding authorities, etc.). Now, likewise, select a point on the internal environment continuum that is reflective of the institution's internal relationships (existing students, Board of Trustees, faculty, staff, etc.). The latter may not be so easily conceptualized since the individual elements are themselves component parts of the institution. Perhaps picturing how these groups view the college would help.

Now, connect the points with a straight line. The line quite naturally intersects the institutional goals continuum at some point. In the model, this point of intersection represents the college's level of effectiveness. In truth, though an institution's mission may be unquestionably virtuous, it can rise no higher in its quest of excellence than its relationships will allow. In this context, establishing and maintaining positive external and internal relationships well may be a most appropriate definition of governance.

One does not have to "buy into" the notion that the community college mission is cast in concrete to appreciate the implications of viewing governance as a relational activity. Three key subsets of the governance theme are organizational structure, management style and finance. Each is examined here in the context of external and internal relationships in an effort to isolate future implications that are useful to community college managers.

Organizational Structure

Public policy is evolutionary and community college leaders today constantly must be aware of the directional changes happening in the marketplace. Zammuto (1982) said that an organization can be termed as effective if it is, by the client's definition, meeting his demands satisfactorily. An effective organization must change as client needs change if it is to remain effective.

The rapidly changing environment that institutions of higher learning are facing may indicate that more consideration should be focused on the concept of "organizational adaptation." Kim Cameron, (1984) director of the Organizational Studies Program at the National Center for Higher Education Management Systems, defines organizational adaptation as the "modifications and alterations in the organization or its components in order to adjust to changes in the equilibrium to an imbalanced condition . . . the emphasis is definitely on responding to some discontinuity or lack of fit that arises between the organization and its environment." Cameron refers to a "life cycles" approach to adaptation in which organizations are assumed to progress through four sequential stages of development. Perhaps community colleges are beginning to enter the fourth stage of development in which decentralization, domain expansion and renewed adaptability take place and new subsystems are established. During this stage the problem is to overcome inflexibility and conservatism, and expand to meet the new client demands.

In other words, community colleges have become "maintenance organizations" and need to strive to become "developmental organizations." Many authorities believe that to truly become developmental institutions, community colleges must establish linkages with the public and private organizations in their service area. Alfred (1984) recently said in an unpublished concept paper that linkages will provide the means for community colleges to regain the "institutional uniqueness" which they once enjoyed but now has become a concept of the past. Dale Parnell (1984) in a recent interview said that linkages with the public schools, the four-year colleges and universities and business and industry "will be the name of the game for the next fifteen years."

With these thoughts in mind community college leaders will have to make their organizational structure flexible enough to deal with the external factors which will be confronting them. The ability of leaders to make the necessary structural changes so that institutional personnel can be best utilized in a manner commensurate with their abilities will become important in achieving organizational effectiveness.

Organization charts in many community colleges and technical institutes have undergone major revisions in the past few years due to the "lack of fit" between the external and/or internal factors. In some instances the organization chart of community colleges is beginning to resemble that of the private colleges or proprietary schools. For example, the positions of resource development officer and public information officer have long been prominent in private colleges and proprietary schools. However, until the past few years, such positions were rarely found on the organization chart of a community college. But times have changed. With federal, state and local governments spending less dollars on education, it has become necessary for the community colleges and technical institutes to consider external sources other than governmental agencies for supplemental funding. In order to do this, these institutions have established a position for resource development.

While recruiting students and image building have long been functions that have existed in community colleges, these responsibilities were usually assigned to a staff member who had other primary responsibilities. Many community colleges recently have upgraded the importance of these responsibilities by hiring a full-time public information/public relations officer.

In a June 1984 personal interview, Dale Parnell, president of the American Association of Colleges and Junior Colleges, stressed the importance of image building by the community colleges. He said that too many people have a fuzzy image of the community college. He thinks these colleges should become very serious in their attempt to clarify this image in the public's eyes. Parnell sees image building as one of the top challenges facing community colleges as they move toward the year 2000.

Piedmont Technical College is one such institution that has some very noticeable changes in its organizational structure. The changes made are certainly unique to the North Carolina community college system. But with the sweeping changes in the *external* environment, similar forms of organizational adaptation may soon be more prevalent nationwide.

The president of Piedmont Technical College in North Carolina, Dr. Edward Cox (1984), realized the need to have more direct coordination between his institution and the State Department of Commerce, the Department of Labor, the Industrial Services of the State Department of Community Colleges, and local industries in his college's service area in order to solve local manpower problems and meet local manpower training needs. He also wanted to establish more direct communications between the college and the local Chamber of Commerce, Employment Security Commission and the local Economic Development Commission for the purpose of coordinating a search for new industry and for organizing manpower development programs.

The president decided that if he was going to establish better linkages with these agencies then he would need to do a good job in the area of public relations. He also realized that more resources would have to be uncovered to fund these new programs, because his present allocations would not be sufficient for such an expansion in training programs.

In order to accomplish these objectives, a new division was formed in the college and entitled the Office of College Relations and Development. This division consists of a vice-president, two directors and a secretary. The division head answers directly to the president.

The head of this division, who is called Vice-President of College Relations and Development, in addition to his supervisory responsibilities has other assigned duties which include establishing and maintaining direct contact with local businesses and industries to assist them with their training and educational needs.

The Director of Resource Development is responsible for writing grant proposals for federal, state and private funds; organizing and coordinating fund raising activities of the PTC Foundation; and serves as Executive Director of the PTC Foundation. This person is also responsible for all alumni relations and coordinates the annual campus fund drive.

The Director of Public Relations is in charge of writing and coordinating with the area media all of the college's news releases, and is responsible for all the planning, development and management of all the marketing activities of the college. College brochures, the catalog and other publications also fall under the jurisdiction of this position.

After two years of having this new organization in effect, President Cox said that it has proven to be efficient and effective in meeting the needs of the college community. New linkages have been formed between the college and community industries and other agencies; and the response time to community requests has been shortened considerably.

One internal factor which is currently impacting the organizational structure of community colleges is the addition of computers and word processing systems. Leaders should be concerned that information be able to flow up and down through all levels of the organization so that all personnel can obtain the needed information and distribute it to others as the need arises.

Keller (1983) said that information about the internal operations of a college are vital (i.e., space utilization, facility and equipment needs, utility requirements, auditorium, bookstore, etc.). "Improving the management information system," he said, "is therefore an indispensable step in improving the everyday operation of the campus . . ." Parnell said that we must find a way to take the new information available and put it to use in the classroom. Alfred (1984) in a recent classroom lecture said that organization structure should be designed to allow for decentralization of information. Too often the structure makes information available only to the president.

The organizational structure that is conducive to a two-way flow of information provides a context for change, which allows for creative and innovative responses to the external environment.

Management Style

As previously mentioned, in order to develop alternative sources of funding, linkages with the community will become more important to community colleges than ever before. In order to establish these linkages, managers will have to assess their staff's skills and abilities so that appropriate people can be assigned the duty of establishing these linkages.

Ellen Chaffee (1984) with the National Center for Higher Education Management Systems said that strategic management involves attuning and reorienting people in the institution to changes in the market demands so the institution can respond to these changes and "maintain . . . the flow of resources from the market to the organization."

Parnell feels that community colleges are "uniquely situated to take the lead in the community in the establishment of linkages." He says that presidents need to assess their own management style in determining what institutional personnel to involve in the linkage process. Many presidents may wish to take the lead in forming linkages; others who are more internally oriented should provide a structure in which someone else has that responsibility. Parnell, in a recent interview, stressed the importance of the community college maintaining internal flexibility. He suggests that managers should follow what he has labeled the "loose-tight principle." (The word "loose" . . . refers to the flexibility in the college. He says that the trend toward less local control is threatening to take away the colleges' flexibility. Managers need to find ways to maintain that flexibility. "Tight" refers to the value system of the college, the college's real beliefs, what it holds tight.)

The manager also must remain flexible when considering the mission and goals of the institution. Managers must be willing to adjust the mission and/or goals if environmental factors indicate that such change is needed. With a changing public policy putting emphasis more on quality than quantity, a good deal of thought must go into evaluating the mission and goals. The open door philosophy puts the emphasis on enrollment when achievement seems to be more in tune with the thinking of legislators and employers. As Richardson (1984) said, a major issue is to decide whether we need "to concentrate on a more limited range of activities with greater attention to program coherence and student progress."

Finance

The Research Triangle Institute recently published a study of the elements involved in the overall development—growth, stability, stagnation, or decline—for colleges and universities that receive substantial federal grants under Title III of the Higher Education Act. One of the study investigators, N.C. State University Associate Vice-Chancellor for Business and Finance, William Jenkins, noted that strong institutions had leadership, specifically presidents, with an "entrepreneurial kind of vision." This kind of vision, tempered with a new level of business pragmatism, will be needed if crucial relationships with existing sources of community college funding are to be maintained and strengthened. Likewise, entrepreneurial vision and business acumen will be required to identify and cultivate new funding linkages.

In dealing with tax levying authorities, leaders again must forge those kinds of win-win relationships that matched open access and comprehensive programming with the political trend toward individual rights and the war on poverty. Recently the match has been technical training and economic growth. Tomorrow's match may not even be evident today. Herein lies the entrepreneurial challenge. Identify the match, sell it with enthusiasm, let the politician have the credit, and reap the financial benefits for the institution. The formula has worked before; it will work again.

Chaffee (1984) has said that the '80's are bringing the deregulation of higher education. With deregulation always comes opportunities for the new kid on the block. Community colleges with entrepreneurial vision are proving that foundations and private donors are no longer the exclusive domain of independent colleges and large research-based universities.

Contrary to popular myth, all community college alumni are not employed at minimum wage and incapable of being financial supporters. Efforts at establishing fruitful linkages here require proper organization, persistence and, of course, the entrepreneurial vision.

Creative community college financiers may find that tuition and fees can yield additional revenues without the negative effects most educators always assume. Frederick Turk of the accounting firm of Peat, Marwick, Mitchell and Company says, "Pricing strategy has not received enough attention in recent times . . . Many institutions (and systems) actually back into price once the cost budget is established and other revenue estimates are made. In essence, the price (i.e., tuition and fees) is a balancing figure. " Concepts like "demand-based pricing," "price-discrimination strategy," and "competition-based pricing" may seem foreign to community college financiers. So did other marketing terms like "positioning" and "market segmentation" that are now in the vocabulary of most admission officers. Breneman and Nelson (1981) hit hard at pricing considerations with their equity vs. efficiency themes. To them marriage to the old across-the-board-rock-bottom-pricing structures is theoretically inequitable and inefficient. Beyond theory, such a pricing strategy can be downright costly.

Other creative financing arrangements that involve parties not heretofore seen as partners with community colleges are being struck. Imaginative leasing arrangements that allow non-profit entities to "tie-in" to the tax advantages available to private business are an example. College-established foundations with financial flexibilities not allowed within the institution have proven useful at many institutions. Other such linking mechanisms will be devised. The key is vision, entrepreneurial vision.

Perhaps the external relationship that holds the most promise for profitable cultivation by community colleges is that with business and industry. "The total budgets for training and development in business and industry now run about $80-100 billion per year," according to Samuel Dunn (1983). "Traditional teaching institutions will not have a monopoly on higher education," he continues. The question may be whether business and industry will be higher education's competitors or its compatriots. The answer lies again in successful linkage. Parnell is a champion of the business and industry linkage. He is convinced that community colleges have the flexibility to deliver what business and industry need in an era of rapid change. Flexibility is a vital word in the entrepreneur's vocabulary.

The one element that is ever present with the entrepreneur is risk. Vaughan, true to his mission arguments, warns of the "inherent dangers when an academic institution enters into a relationship with other agencies." Institutional integrity is at stake. In each instance, the risk of compromising mission (the goal achievement form of effectiveness) must be balanced against the potentials for achieving effectiveness through linkages with external funding sources.

Having pursued to the maximum all possible sources of funding, community college leadership must then focus inwardly and ask the question, "What is the exact programming mix that will maximize the college's social effectiveness given the practical budget constraints within which it must operate?" There are as many techniques for arriving at answers to this question as there are community colleges. They range from very quantitative and structured mechanisms to very intuitive, "seat of the pants," decision processes.

Whatever the approach, Robert Gruber and Mary Mohr (1983) suggest that it should assist decision makers by:

- encouraging strategic (long-range—what to do) as opposed to tactical (short-range—how to do it) thinking;
- encouraging a holistic, as opposed to anatomistic, viewpoint;
- identifying trade-offs to be considered by program-oriented personnel;
- identifying programs in need of redesign, candidates for expansion or candidates for divestiture;
- suggesting the direction of cash flow among programs; and
- providing broad guidelines for assessing the overall health of an organization.

Gruber and Mohr favor a model which long has been in use by the private sector for "strategic audits," "portfolio management" and "product line pruning." Devised by the Boston Consulting Group, it is known as the "product-portfolio" model. (See Figure 3). After a study of the model, mentally classifying certain traditional community college educational programs should be easy. For example, health occupational programs are most often judged to be highly beneficial for society, yet expensive; Therefore, they will probably rate a negative financial return. These programs fit in the matrix under worthwhile. Note the basic strategy and use of funds suggested in each category.

4-Way Program Classification Model

<table>
<tr>
<td rowspan="2" style="vertical-align: middle">Financial Returns</td>
<td>Positive</td>
<td>Sustaining
(Necessary evil?)

Basic Strategy:
   Maintenance

Use of Funds:*
   Subsidize "worthwhile"
   programs</td>
<td>Beneficial
(Best of all possible worlds)

Basic Strategy:
   Cautious expansion

Use of Funds:
   Trade-off — plowback or
   subsidize "worthwhile"
   programs</td>
</tr>
<tr>
<td>Negative</td>
<td>Detrimental
(No redeeming qualities)

Basic Strategy:
   Pruning

Use of Funds:
   None available</td>
<td>Worthwhile
(Satisfying, good for society)

Basic Strategy:
   Careful nurturing

Use of Funds:
   None available</td>
</tr>
<tr>
<td></td>
<td></td>
<td style="text-align:center">Low</td>
<td style="text-align:center">High</td>
</tr>
</table>

Benefits
(Social Value)

*Refers to internally generated funds.   Figure 3   (Gruber and Mohr 1983)

Keller (1983) has jazzed up this basic model listing the matrix classifications of dogs, stars, cows and "?". The key elements of the matrix are financial returns and benefit or social value. The genius of this model is that it allows complete flexibility to assign values to these two elements, yet it also allows the decision maker to view programming holistically and see the overall effect of making certain trade offs.

What is needed to make this model even better are management tools that assist in the proper classification of programming. The financial returns sector can be reduced to a basic cost vs. revenue analysis. Regrettably most community colleges cannot identify costs, even direct costs, by programs. Perhaps program revenues are more easily identifiable. This is especially true in those colleges which have full-time equivalency funding formulas. Ideally the cost/revenue information should be a product of the institution's accounting operation.

Conceptually, costs and revenues are more readily evaluated than benefits. Some colleges are making great strides in quantifying social benefits. Departments for institutional research can earn their keep in this area. However, the importance of intuition should not be too heavily discounted. Here, true leaders earn their keep.

Gruber and Mohr sum up the need for a cost/benefit analytical approach to programming by concluding "adminstrators and board directors of non-profit organizations will be faced with increasingly severe competition for time, money, and management skills as the non-profit sector becomes more cost conscious. Dedication must be accompanied by performance results, idealism tempered with pragmatism."

IMPLICATIONS

From this examination of the processes of governance, several implications for the future spring forth. In the '80's and beyond, community college leaders who are mindful of these implications will find the seas of higher education no less turbulent but much more navigable than those who are heedless.

- Because of the increasing velocity of changes taking place in the external environment, community colleges will have to regularly alter their organizational structure to remain congruent with public policy.
- Community college leaders, in order to become more efficient and effective from an internal point of view, must find innovative approaches to organizational structure.
- Management strengths and weaknesses of administrators must be assessed so that the college can become more effective in dealing with the external environment.
- Management styles must be flexible in order to avoid internal conflicts that hinder institutional progress.
- Community college leaders need to have an entrepreneurial vision and business pragmatism when dealing with the institution's sources of funding.
- Some mechanism is needed to assist administrators in the process of balancing the social appropriateness of institutional programming with practical budgetary constraints.

CONCLUSION

Colleges need to concern themselves with organizational effectiveness in order to achieve excellence. Richardson's model is presented as a framework for managers to use to renew their thinking on this subject.

More attention needs to be given to the mission of the community college, and Vaughan's educational trends are introduced to help leaders find a perspective around which they can rally to revitalize the mission and to help the colleges maintain institutional integrity.

Based on external and internal environmental factors, a model for organizational effectiveness is offered as a means of assisting institutions in their pursuit of excellence.

Organizational structure needs to be looked at as a concept that can change as the environment dictates. Examples of recent changes in organizational structure are offered as food for thought for educational leaders.

Management styles also need to change to keep pace with other new developments in the education field. Effective leaders will have to come to grips with such concepts as "flexibility" and linkages."

Community colleges will have to show entrepreneurial vision to insure adequate funding for the colleges in the years ahead. With deregulation, community colleges will have to depend more on private sources for their monetary needs.

Reviewers for this Chapter

Charles E. Taylor, Jr.
Vice President for Business and
    Finance
Meredith College
Raleigh, North Carolina

Thomas B. Anderson
Dean of Student Services
Edgecombe Technical College
Tarboro, North Carolina

REFERENCES

Alfred, R. L. "Changing Patterns of Governance." Paper presented at North Carolina State University, Raleigh, North Carolina, July 1984.

Baker, G. A., III, and T. Thompson. "Coping with Complexity: A Challenge for Open-Door Colleges." *Community College Frontiers* 9, no. 2 (Winter 1981): 26-32.

Breneman, D. W., and S. C. Nelson. *Financing Community Colleges: An Economic Perspective.* Washington, D.C.: The Brookings Institution, 1981.

Cameron, K. S. "Organizational Adaptation and Higher Education." *Journal of Higher Education* 55, no. 2 (March/April 1984): 122-44.

Chaffee, E. E. "Successful Strategic Management in Small Private Colleges." *Journal of Higher Education* 55, no. 2 (March/April 1984): 212-41.

Cohen, A. M., and F. B. Brawer. *The American Community College.* San Francisco: Jossey-Bass, 1982.

Cox, E. Telephone Interview by Thomas B. Anderson, 9 July 1984.

Davis, J. R., R. Ironside and J. V. Sant. "Leadership Planning: Keys to Strong Colleges." *Hypotenuse.* Research Triangle Institute (March/April 1984): 4-5.

Dunn, S. L. "The Changing University: Survival in the Information Society." *The Futurist* 17, no. 4, (August 1983): 55-60.

Gronn, P. C. "On Studying Administrators at Work." *Educational Administration Quarterly* 20, no. 1 (Winter 1984): 115-19.

Gruber, R., and M. Mohr. "Strategic Management for Multiprogram Non-profit Organizations." *California Management Review* (Spring 1982).

Keller, G. *Academic Strategy, The Management Revolution in Higher Education.* Baltimore: Johns Hopkins University Press, 1983.

Mayhew, B. *Surviving the Eighties.* San Francisco: Jossey-Bass, 1979.

Miles, R. H. *Macro-Organizational Behavior.* Glenview, Ill.: Scott, Foresman, 1980.

Mintzberg, J. *The Nature of Managerial Work.* New York: Harper and Row, 1973.

_____.*The Structuring of Organizations: A Synthesis of the Research.* Englewood Cliffs, N.J.: Prentice-Hall, 1979.

National Commission on Excellence in Education. *A Nation at Risk: The Imperative for Educational Reform.* Washington, D.C.: Government Printing Office, 1983.

Parnell, D. "Opportunity with Excellence: Vision of the Future." Interview by Dale F. Campbell and Robert M. Stivender, 13 June 1984. Tape recording, American Association of Community and Junior Colleges, Washington, D.C.

Reddin, W. J. *Managerial Effectiveness.* New York: McGraw-Hill, 1970.

Richardson, R. C. Jr. "Tipping the Scales from Growth to Achievement: Community College Leadership in the Eighties." *ACCT Trustee Quarterly* 7, no. 3 (Summer 1983a): 22-25.

_____. "Open Access and Institutional Policy: Time for Re-examination." *Community College Review* 10, no. 4 (Spring 1983b): 47-51.

_____. "Finance and Governance." Paper presented at the Presidents' Leadership Institute, Asheville-Buncombe Technical College, Asheville, North Carolina, December 1983c.

_____. "Management Challenges: Principles and Strategies for the 1980s." In *Emerging Roles for Community College Leaders.* New Directions for Community Colleges, no. 46, San Francisco: Jossey-Bass, 1984: 21-31.

Roueche, J. E., and G. A. Baker III. *Beacons for Change: An Innovative Outcome Model for Community Colleges.* Iowa City, Iowa: American College Testing Program, 1983.

Turk, F. "New Initiatives for Management: Increasing Revenues and Resources." *Business Officer* 17, no. 11 (May 1984): 17-32.

Vaughan, G. B. and Associates. *Issues for Community College Leaders in a New Era*. San Francisco: Jossey-Bass, 1983.

Vaughan, G. B. "Finance and Governance." Paper presented at the Presidents' Leadership Institute, Asheville-Buncombe Technical College, Asheville, North Carolina, December 1983.

_____. "Balancing Open Access and Quality, The Community College at the Watershed." *Change* 16, no. 3 (April 1984): 38-44.

Zammuto, R. F. *Assessing Organizational Effectiveness*. Albany: State University of New York Press, 1982.

Chapter 3

LEADERSHIP AND THE CURRICULUM

Researcher,
John E. Roueche,
Professor and Director,
Program in Community College
  Education
The University of Texas at Austin

Practitioner,
Thomas E. Barton,
President
Greenville Technical College
Greenville, South Carolina

Principal Resource Persons Reviewed in this Chapter

RATIONALE

Leadership is caring about and attending to the quality of the institution . . . Quality is not what students have when they come to college but what they possess when they leave. What have students accomplished at the end of the education process? Are they literate—can they read—can they write—can they problem solve? Do they have good job skills? Do employers say, "Your graduates are the best prepared I know. —I prefer your graduate to any others?" Quality examines what students came to learn, and how well they do compared to others who studied elsewhere.

John E. Roueche

When talking about the emerging technologies, the first thing is to identify the job needs in your area. That is something that constantly changes, and something we have to say in tune with all the time. New industry coming in, old industry modifying what they're doing, retooling their equipment, and reshaping their whole approach to what they're doing—all of this is going on all the time in industry. How do we keep up with all that? You're too involved with board meetings, internal staff problems, court cases, and other things that tie up your time.

Thomas E. Barton

OBJECTIVES

By the end of this chapter the reader should be able to:
1. Discuss leadership strategies to ensure quality in the instructional effort.
2. Understand the process of the community college instructional program as a linking pin.
3. Discuss the diversity of inputs and need to keep output (excellence) relevent to community needs.
4. Relate strategies used at other institutions to structure an instructional program that makes good on the promise of community college mission to the environment.

INTRODUCTION

Among the goals of the North Carolina Presidents' Leadership Institute was to acquire new skills and strategies to update occupational programs. To this end the Institute invited one of the leading researchers on community college leadership, Dr. John E. Roueche from the University of Texas in Austin. Dr. Roueche's comments centered around leadership strategies to help faculty and students achieve their potentials. This session also highlighted Dr. Tom Barton, President of Greenville Technical College in Greenville, South Carolina. Dr. Barton shared several strategies practiced at his institution that have contributed to its success.

Opportunity refers to access or the open door, the founding principle of the community college movement. According to Dale Parnell (1984b) excellence is for and about not who is enrolled but what happened to them during their stay and where they stood when they left, regardless of when they left. Then opportunity is the community college input; excellence, the output. The process, that which transforms input to output, is learning facilitated by the instructional program. To achieve excellence the instructional program must itself have the characteristics of excellence and be responsive to changing community needs. Excellence in instructional programs allows the community college to achieve "Opportunity with Excellence." Success must be measured by the success of graduates and "stop-in/stop-out" students. Do they get jobs? Are they admitted and do they succeed in four-year colleges? The bottom line is where they stand when they leave (Parnell 1984b).

To achieve excellence during times of adversity as well as prosperity, community college leadership must determinedly and boldly develop and employ strategies to support quality and relevancy in the instructional program. Good managers, indeed all managers, at the community college level had better be highly supportive of the major product, learning (Parnell 1984b). The community colleges' success with facilitating learning will achieve excellence. This chapter will discuss leadership and curriculum strategies designed to help achieve learning, and help ensure that the instructional program responds to a dynamic environment. Internal factors contributing to excellence that will be discussed include dealing with the diversity in the abilities of new students, demanding excellence in teaching and demanding excellence from students. External factors focus on building linkages with high schools, employers, area four-year colleges and universities.

Researcher

At the President's Leadership Institute, Dr. Roueche discussed with North

Leadership Strategies for Community College Effectiveness

Carolina presidents several issues and strategies to help achieve excellence. The following is a topical review and synthesis of his remarks:

Leadership. Leadership is caring about and attending to the quality of the institution. Leaders must really care about what goes on in the organization. If one does not care about the quality of the enterprise it will not happen. Mediocrity will be the end result. In caring, one must have high expectations for faculty and students. Signaling expectations (caring) may be as simple as asking the right questions. Asking people about their work communicates interest and care and can effect powerful results within the educational institution. Dr. Roueche stated: "In the past year, I've visited and interviewed faculty in over one hundred community colleges. I asked them how often the department chairperson or dean met with the faculty to talk about quality or other classroom procedures. Their responses almost always were negative. Faculty perception is that no one cares about these matters. The dean is too busy with the catalog, scheduling and other administrative concerns. Not that these are unimportant, but deans and department heads, being quality control agents, should be devoting 90% of their time to improving instruction. I think that for the past 20 years we have suffered from leaderlessness in education." For example, Presidents also must attend to excellence. A college president in Arizona sent a memo to all division chairs stating his concern over the quality of written work in all college courses. He asked them to send him samples of written work from all courses. Rumors then reached him that many instructors had not previously required written assignments and now were making such assignments to have samples for the president. Therefore, written work rose dramatically. Without an edict or formal policy, the president signaled his care about and expectations in the classroom proceedings.

Teaching. College leadership must set high expectations for the faculty. To ignore bad behavior anywhere is to encourage it. For instance, voluntary staff development is found only in colleges. Private industry requires that its personnel stay abreast of changes and be prepared for the future. To expect faculty to do the same, voluntarily, is a low-level expectation. Leaders in this effort must practice leadership by example. When administrators miss professional development activities it creates a perception among the faculty that the activity is not important.

Two years ago, University of Texas at Austin completed a study of teaching in eleven Texas community college campuses. The findings were alarming. Half of the teachers did not make regular assignments in the textbook. There were almost no written assignments and little or no homework required. Test questions were almost always straight from the lecture. Leadership must demand that instructors expect learning quantity and quality from students.

To improve teaching one must examine what transpires in the classroom, and indicate expectations of excellence. College leaders should make known to the faculty their expectations about teaching. To accomplish this leaders again must ask the right questions. By asking about attrition, class assignments, evaluation procedures and job placement success, leadership demonstrates its expectations of the instructional effort and its caring about the quality of instruction. Quality must be celebrated. Excellence in teaching must be rewarded by giving excellent teachers money, awards, bringing them before the board, putting their pictures in the newspapers, etc. The allure of pride and respect that once brought good people into teaching despite low pay must return. The job of the leader is to excite people to potentials they have never thought of and realizatons they have never dared to dream of themselves. Leaders must get the organization to reflect the very best that they expect it to be. People want to be associated with quality. Parnell (1984b) envisions a community college faculty that will view the community college as the premier teaching assignment in higher education.

The other side of high expectations is supporting, reinforcing, and rewarding as those expectations are reached. If there is excellence it should be recognized, rewarded and celebrated. Let the people who do a good job know they are valued. *In Search of Excellence: Lessons from America's Best Run Companies* is a most exciting book. Every president, dean, and department head should read it. According to the authors, Peters and Waterman (1982) the best companies are built on people not management theories or formulas. The best companies do many little things that symbolize quality in the organization. We live in a society where competition and success is very powerful, and people like to be recognized as winners. I.B.M., for example, rents the Meadowlands Stadium in New Jersey, hires the Rutgers University Marching Band, and lets a hundred of their top performers run in under the goalposts with the band playing and their names appearing on the scoreboard. Other top companies give out lapel ribbons or buttons. The whole idea is to celebrate excellence.

Students. The community college product is learning. Too often education becomes process oriented. Library books and the square feet in a building are counted, the credentials of faculty are examined, average salaries are calculated, etc. The hope in conclusions from these variables is having a quality institution. The assumption is that people who completed a course must have learned something; and if they complete enough courses they get a degree, diploma or certificate. But this process is no guarantee of quality. Quality focuses on what students learn and achieve. Leaders must communicate to students that they expect them to excell. Everyone wants to be associated with excellence, including students. An example is the Miami-Dade Community College reform called the Standards of Academic Progress. Through this program the college expresses its expectations for performance by students. The program provides a system of warning, probation and suspension of students failing to meet expectations. McCabe and Skidmore (1983) report that students now are performing at higher achievement rates in order to continue at the college. That Miami-Dade and other community colleges are now reporting better retention to the associate degree and certificates is an example of what can happen when expectations about quality in the classroom are tough. Best of all, these reports show an almost straight line improvement in achievement in almost every curriculum area.

The open door policy assures a wide range of academic abilities among students who enter. At the same time, there is only so much diversity a teacher can accomodate without giving up quality. To help learners toward their goals, recognizing what the academic abilities of entering students are, and devising strategies in helping them succeed, is necessary. Determining the abilities of entering students becomes increasingly difficult. As the National Commission on Excellence in Education report suggests the meaning of a high school diploma has changed. In 1970, the average high school graduate had a C+ grade point average, representing a slightly better than tenth grade reading level. In 1983, according to the National Assessment of Educational Progress, the average high school graduate had a B to B+ average possessing less than eight grade reading ability. High school grade point averages are no longer a reliable predictor of success, and there is a continuing general decline in college readiness by high school graduates. At the same time, a readability study of the textbooks used at

Riverside Community College in California found that only one course in a hundred used reading material below the twelfth grade level. Therefore, if students with eighth grade reading levels enter these college courses, they do not have a prayer for success if quality is required.

Testing at admissions, not for the purpose of selection but for the purpose of assessment and placement, must be done to accomodate diversity. Baker and Thompson (1981) call for restructuring the college to better manage diversity and complexity and to make the implied promise of open admissions one that yields success in much greater numbers than are currently being documented in American community colleges. They urge for the creation of "buffers" to reduce the diversity of students entering curricula. The first buffer is the college's assessment center. The second buffer is a remedial or developmental studies program. In 1978, Miami-Dade Community College began its reform of the educational program. One of the primary thrusts of the reform was for the college to become more directive. In this more directive system, students with deficiencies were required to take necessary developmental work before proceeding to programs where the lack of skill could cause failure (McCabe 1981). The reforms are beginning to show results. According to McCabe and Skidmore (1983) students improve performance, increase completion rates and G. P. A. and have lower suspension rates when they are informed early of deficiencies and avail themselves of needed special assistance.

Presidential Practitioner

Dr. Tom Barton has been very active in what Dale Parnell (1984b) predicts will be the name of the game for community colleges for the next 15 years, building linkages. As president of Greenville Technical College, Dr. Barton has built strong linkages with area high schools, employers and four-year colleges. In the following, discussion Dr. Barton shares some of his successful strategies in linkage building, and discusses some of the advantages strong linkage building has brought to Greenville Technical College.

1. Linkages to High Schools

During the next several years, the number of high school graduates is going to decline. This means doing a better job than ever in recruiting high school graduates or facing declining budgets. Greenville TEC had developed a marketing plan which is an annual strategy for reaching high school graduates and other learners. Those on staff who are responsible for this plan's implementation are accountable for the results, and their monthly reports are reviewed to determine the progress being made.

With frequent personal visits, newsletters and other materials, a recruiting team works constantly to keep high school counselors aware of what is happening on the Greenville TEC campus. These counselors must know as much about the college as the college staff does.

There must be productivity in education just as in industry, and through careful evaluation of these activities, that productivity can be determined.

2. Developmental Education

When high school graduates come to a community college, about 40% of them are at an eighth grade reading and mathematics level. These people lack the basic skills for a high tech curriculum. Instead of turning them away, Greenville TEC chose to accept the goal of building the best developmental or remedial program in the nation. Today, that program exists. Each month, 95 to 100 people complete their developmental education and are qualified to enter the curriculum program of their choice. That means that people will be prepared to get better jobs than they otherwise could have had.

The developmental program undergirds the entire operation. Without it, the institution will not be complete.

3. Linkages with Employers

Business and industry is constantly changing, and each community exists in its own environment with its own unique job needs. Several years ago, Greenville TEC searched for a means to keep up with local business and industry. They looked at the expanding role and the benefits from advisory committees, and decided to rebuild and revise the network of committees. The results were rewarding.

These committees use their expertise to help the college develop and revise curricula, ensuring that students learn the right things. They help to evaluate faculty and aid in faculty development through return-to-industry programs and other activities. They help to assess equipment needs and have contributed some $4 million in equipment acquisitions in just 15 months. Their interest in students is evidenced by strong job placement support and by raising some $250,000 in student scholarships.

In building this strong network of committees, Greenville TEC realized the necessity of employing a full-time director. The director's role is to coordinate and provide leadership to the 50-plus advisory committees that are involved with the college. This director is responsible for scheduling meetings, preparing agendas, keeping official minutes, rotating memberships, ensuring open communications between administration and the committees, and timely reporting of findings. The director also develops a handbook, an annual directory, and a quarterly newsletter.

An annual plan for all committees is prepared, outlining responsibilities. The major responsibility is an annual report on programs with which the committees are involved. These evaluations focus on curriculum, faculty, equipment facilities, public relations, and employment outlooks. Comments and suggestions are made for improvement, change or even for termination of programs, as their studies of internal and external factors indicate.

A representative of each division of study then reports the results of these evaluations to a Program Review Committee made up of three members of the Greenville TEC Board. The reports become guidelines for budget priorities and even employment decisions. They are studied by college officials who follow through on suggestions and report on action taken.

For committee membership, the college looks for people with both knowledge in their fields and political influence. Keep in mind that to have a strong committee one needs to have people with the right skills for the curriculum being studied. For example, in high-tech curricula, do not necessarily invite the president of the company or his officers. Instead, select engineers and front-line production people who know the jobs and the skills required for those jobs.

With more than 500 people serving on these committees, Greenville TEC also creates strong community support. By exciting these people about the college, their influence on local and state funding sources and in other vital areas is obtained.

Advisory committee membrs also help with a program called DACUM (Developing a Curriculum), which helps the institution develop new curricula or update older ones. Members frequently participate in DACUM workshops or find others to serve. In these workshops, people who perform a job are brought on campus to compose a chart describing general areas of competence and necessary skills. This chart becomes the basis for curriculum development, a competency check list for students, a career guidance tool and a job placement tool. (Faculty members are not included in a DACUM, in order to ensure that all involved will be objective about changing a curriculum.)

Greenville TEC, seeks other ways to build linkages with business and industry. In high-tech education, the present state is not enough. Industry will undergo even more rapid changes in the future than in the recent past, and they will be depending on the community colleges to stay up to date with and to be ahead of the state of the art. In this regard, Greenville TEC is becoming the research center for the State of South Carolina in machine tooling and in compurter-controlled equipment. The college will be tied closely with companies at the drawing board stage, instead of later when a new technology affects the market. Projects such as this greatly improve the esteem of the college in the community.

4. Linkages to Four-Year Institution

In 1978, local industry began to tell Greenville TEC that two-year training for technicians was not enough. To respond to this concern, Greenville invited Clemson University to teach the final two years of a four-year degree program in engineering technology on the Greenville TEC campus. Today, one can begin in Greenville in development education and continue through a four-year degree in engineering programs, computer science, other technician programs and other programs supported by several universities. Greenville TEC is actually developing a "university center" where any university can provide four-year programs and beyond. Entrance into highly sophisticated technology fields without strong collegiate studies in English, science, or mathematics is impossible. A strong collegiate program enhances the entire institution.

This effort to build a working linkage with four-year colleges and universities has paid excellent benefits, and Greenville TEC is held in even higher regard by area business and industry and the community as a whole.

IMPLICATIONS

In studying attempts by selected private colleges to deal with decline, Ellen Chaffee (1984) identified two strategic models. The first was the adaptive model, which involves atuning the organization to changes in market demands. This strategy is being expertly fine tuned by the efforts of Tom Barton. The second strategy discussed by Chaffee is the interpretive model, which accepts that an organization is a network of individuals, and a key leadership role is to assure the management of meaning or focus on mission. This model is reflected in Dale Parnell's (1984b) belief that the community college must adopt a "loose-tight" principle. They must be "loose" on flexibility of programs, and on allowing creativity from faculties. To ensure that faculty efforts (indeed the efforts of all the college's personnel) are directed toward desired goals they must be "tight" about what they believe in, mission. The successful colleges in Chaffee's study are those that found their own unique blend of the adaptive and the interpretive. Administrators should use an interpretive model of strategy without forgetting the demands of their constituents. When a proposal for a new high-demand program is presented, the burden of proof should be on the proposer to show that the program expresses the institution's mission (Chaffee 1984). Hence, curriculum grows out of mission.

Roueche (1984) believes that by-and-large clarity on mission is not common in educational organizations. Leadership must ensure that everyone is clear, at all times, as to the mission of the college. In this effort leaders must rely on their skills as educators. Some people have found something negative about promoting excellent educators into positions of leadership. This strong ability to teach can be one of leadership's most effective tools to achieve success. The concept of the leader as a teacher is finding its way into industry as reported by Douglas Williams (1983). "The predominant style of leadership has gone through three stages. In the first stage, the leader was a man on a horse leading the troops. This gave way to the view of the leader as a leader of leaders. We are now passing into still a third stage in which the top people in an organization have to be the teachers of the leaders under them. The leader as a teacher is a concept that has many significant implications." Williams adds, "The imparting of corporate values-setting the example-has to be carried on throughout the organization by the leaders of the various segments of the business." This is not to say that a person from a non-teaching background can not be a good educational leader. Explaining that business managers make good presidents, Campbell (1983b) states that the key is to be problem oriented (ask the right questions). John Roueche's remarks explain this power.

Leaders must adopt the interpretive model or strategy, but must also be experts at adaptive strategy as well. To do so they must build strong linkages to their communities. There are many objectives in establishing linkages with external institutions. First, strengthen the curricula. By knowing about the characteristics of area high schools one can more accurately adapt the organizations's instructional program to fit the needs of incoming students, an opportunity to practice what Peters and Waterman (1982) call "stay close to the customer." By understanding the needs and operations of area employers leaders can more accurately focus learning on the right things. By articulating clearly with four year colleges in the service area they can devise curricula that help the transfer student transfer more credits, and enrich his or her opportunity to succeed at the baccalaureate level. Parnell (1984b) would like to see our college transfer program be so good that there would never be a question about a student transfering a credit from a community college.

Second, by the image we project when building linkages we want to enhance our graduates ability to find employment or achieve success at transfering. We must project our committment to excellence, and build public confidence in what we do. Third, we want these organizations to not only help us build successful curricula and accept our graduates, but to also become a source of part-time instructors, partners in professional exchange, donors to foundations, and partners in establishing new linkages. Fourth, we want the linkages to be continuous. As communities change the community college curricula must also change to be viable in the future. In establishing linkages we must also utilize all the personnel of the college. The image of the president as Mr. or Ms. "Outside," and all others going about the internal affairs of the college must end to achieve the spectrum of linkages needed to excell. Campbell (1983a) sees a future for community colleges in which the faculty will build networks (linkages) with area computer users to organize and disseminate the resource of the information age, knowledge. This kind of networking requires that all of the college must be prepared and capable of establishing and maintaining linkages.

We must believe in and develop partnerships in learning excellence with our high school colleagues. An exciting approach to this kind of linkage is the "two plus two tech-prep" curriculum (Parnell 1984a). This program would begin in the junior year of high school and culminate at the community college. Such a program may provide goals for those high school students who do not choose traditional "college-prep" programs. By emphasizing applied science, applied math, and literacy students may develop a greater appreciation for and higher achievement in these areas. Increasing an enthusiasm for learning "tech-prep" would broaden not narrow horizons for students. To deepen the linkage with high schools, community colleges also can utilize their strength of flexibility to assist with teacher renewal. Community colleges are in prime position to develop and deliver programs for public school teachers in areas like math and science, and at times convenient to those teachers. Helping high schools strive for excellence could pay dividends far sooner than would a national effort to attract new teachers to these disciplines (Gordon 1983).

Linkages to employers may be one of the most important efforts undertaken by a community college. Serving as a linking pin between current job readiness and employer needs is the primary role of most community colleges. Concern for the needs of area employers establishes a confidence in programs, colleges, and most importantly graduates. Advisory Committees as developed by Dr. Barton should be the cornerstone of an effective linkage effort, but already established links for other purposes can be used to strengthen the total effort. One such opportunity is with Cooperative Education. The benefits to the student and participating employer in Cooperative Education are numerous. In establishing a student in a cooperative education position, the college is helping to link the student to his or her goals of meaningful employment. It is also an effective linkage for the instructional program to employers. According to Salisbury (1977) the community college is an extension of the community it serves; therefore, cooperative education is often the source for public contact. "Public image" is vitally important and feedback is necessary. Not only must the community support the college, but the college must be responsive to the needs of the community. The close monitoring of student placements and business community contacts can lead to course revisions and deletions, as well as institution of new programs. The link to employers who are hiring students for cooperative education positions becomes a vehicle for the college to ask if the student was well prepared. By establishing this linkage the college may also reduce the need to race with the state of the art in purchasing equipment. By clearly establishing with Cooperative Education employers what the college will teach and what the employer will train will reduce the need to have every new technology while providing a complete instructional program to the student. In a time of limited resources, should community college leadership give priority to the acquisition of new equipment (things) or promoting faculty acquisition of new information (knowledge) (Campbell 1983a)?

Not only must community colleges be adept at building linkages, but when they do have the necessary data to make decisions about the instructional program they must be able to act. According to Peters and Waterman (1982) the excellent companies are those that have an action orientation. While explaining why employement in the U.S. has been rising faster than that of Europe, Bernd Hof of the IW-Research Institute in Cologne stated that the turnover rate of labor in American industry is about twice as high as in Germany-a sign of rapid innovation. That new jobs in America are created primarily in small and medium-sized firms is significant. There is more room for private initiative and aggressive forward strategies. To be successful at satisfying the employment needs of industry, community colleges must be equally innovative and as aggressive. The place to allow this entrepreneurship may be the Continuing Education or Extension division. This division can adopt Peters and Waterman's "do it-fix it-try it" approach to developing courses and programs. In this regard, the Continuing Education division would become the path finder for curriculum programs that grow out of their success.

Harris and Grede (1977) abstracted three levels of competence from *Individualized Educational Planning*, a 1975 study by Metropolitan State University in St. Paul. They are as follows:

> *Knowing*: To know means to have *learned and retained* and *be able to recall* the theory and methodology . . . and the context of a particular subject.
> *Applying*: To apply means to be able and willing to *use* the theory and methodology . . . and the context of a subject in new and routine situations.
> *Evaluating*: To evaluate means to be able to *judge the value* of theory and methodology . . . and context of the subject in relation to goals or stated criteria. The evaluation process implies an informed judgement.

Based on these levels of competency, Harris and Grede provide a guide to developing curricula that encourages the achievement of these levels. "Theoretical and Background" courses should be part of a curriculum to help students achieve the knowing level. "Specialized Occupational" courses should be included to help students reach the applying or hands on level. Finally, "General Education" courses must be made a part of the curriculum to help students achieve the evaluating level. By adding the skills and attitudes necessary to problem solve and learn independently, the community college helps the student prepare for what is beyond the entry level job. Owen (1984) states that without question, the rapidity with which change is occuring in industry-processes, machines and management-change that creates positions overnight and eliminates others during the same period-is evidence that broad general education skills are needed to continue to *hold* a job, to move into *new* jobs and to *change* careers. Part of the value of general education today may be instilling in adults a commitment to *lifelong learning*-to continually come back for development and refreshment-just to keep up with today's advancements.

Unfortunately, many students have a negative view of general education requirements. Freqently, they are taken with the attitude of "getting them out of the way," or they are skipped in the curriculum with the student taking only the knowing and applying level courses to get to the job market as fast as possible. To address this problem, Rippey and Campbell (1982) outline the strategy devised at Vernon Regional Junior College in Texas. The Catalog and Curriculum Committee decided that once students enrolled in their occupational specialization, proper academic advising and experience would eventually convince them of the need for competencies in general education courses. In the interim, the college's responsibility was to assist each student in developing their full potential and a genuine love for learning. Then, if students did "stop-out" for whatever reason, they would eventually want to return to continue career development.

In general the program at Vernon accepts the principles of lifelong learning and career laddering. Certificate programs, eliminating general education courses, were set up, including courses in technical competencies (knowing and applying levels) and electives. These electives include three new courses.

1. Career Development Competencies for career exploration and decisionmaking.
2. Occupational Adjustment for pre-employment/pre-supervised work experience.
3. Supervised Work Experience/Cooperative Education.

These electives are an attempt to respond to employer priorities relating to getting to work on time, getting along with co-workers and honesty. After completing the certificate level students may "stop out" with job skills and attitudes conducive to successful employment. If the student choose to "stop in" again, he or she may continue towards an Associate in Applied Science Degree where general education courses are increased. In the appendix is a conceptual model of the reform at Vernon and an explanation of the new courses.

Emerging technologies, high tech industries and information age are terms that imply a future for our students. The growth rate for these high tech industries are impressive. However, Levin and Rumberger (1983) warn that although the growth rates of high tech jobs are high, growth in terms of numbers are in the service industry. *U.S. News and World Report* (1984) in analyzing the 1984-85 *Occupational Outlook Handbook* states that the service industries - including transportation, communications, utilities, finance, insurance, real estate and government - will account for almost 75 percent of all new jobs through 1995 . . . employment in high-technology industries is expected to contribute only a relatively small share of total job growth, accounting for just 6 percent of all new jobs. We must attack with equal vigor (as we do high tech) career preparation in the areas of business and human services. As more couples with children become working couples, they will depend more on child care and other human services previously taken care of in the home. What obligation do we have to our communities to do all we can to ensure that these services will be the best they can be? As Chaffee (1984) endorses, colleges must seek their own unique strategies, and as Gleazer (1980) states, we must be community-oriented.

Implications. The implications for the future leaders of the community college movement are many. The following consideration of only a few of the implications suggest that leaders must:

- Be true to the mission of the college. They should make themselves experts on the mission of the college and become advocates of it, to the students, faculty, and community.
- Reach out to the community utilizing every contact or linkage possible. Utilizing these linkages to develop curricula will make good on the promise of the mission.
- Hire the best possible personnel and expect the most from them. Constantly communicate the expectations of greatness, and reward it with pay and praise.
- Expect greatness from students. Ensure that the disillusionment in the nation's public schools does not extend to the community college movement.

- Prepare people for careers not jobs. This may require creativity and daring in curriculum planning. It may also require unpopular choices as many do not look beyond the entry level job especially when unemployed.

CONCLUSION

- Future leadership must care about their institution's mission, personnel, students and communities. They must also become adept at expressing and demonstrating caring to the point that it becomes infectious. Faculties and support personnel must care about the excellence of their own efforts and the achievement levels of their students. Caring is the motivator; the actual achievement of objectives and the fulfillment of mission requires the development and practice of skills in areas such as needs assessment, linkage building and curriculum design. Skill building in these areas are complicated by the dynamics of communities and macro-environments. To provide instructional programs that make good on the promises of mission statements in community colleges, faculties must develop and maintain knowledges and skills in measuring the changing abilities and needs of entering students (inputs), new technologies in learning (processes), and changing societal demands (outputs). Leadership's responsibilities, therefore, include providing the opportunities for the development of these knowledges and skills and their constant renewal. Community colleges are about the business of learning, and that extends to its personnel as receivers of college sponsored and encouraged learning.

Reviewer for this Chapter

Robert M. Stivender
Dean of Business Education
Wake Technical College
Raleigh, North Carolina

REFERENCES

Baker, G. A., III, and T. R. Thompson. "Coping with Complexity: A Challenge for Open-Door Colleges." *Community College Frontiers* 9, no. 2 (Winter 1981): 26-32.

Barton, T. E., Jr. "Updating Occupational Education Programs for the Emerging Technologies." Paper presented at the Presidents' Leadership Institute, Catawba Valley Technical College, Hickory, North Carolina, March 1984.

Campbell, D. F. "New Challenges for Leadership." *Community College Review* 10, no. 4 (Spring 1983a): 12-17.

_____. "Cruising for Presidential Timber? Businessmen Best." *Community and Junior College Journal* 54, no. 2 (October 1983b): 35-36.

Chaffee, E. E. "Successful Strategic Management in Small Private Colleges." *Journal of Higher Education* 55, no.2 (March/April, 1984): 212-41.

Greenville Technical College. *Advisory Committees.* Greenville, S.C.: Greenville Technical College, n.d.

Harris, N. C., and J. F. Grede. *Career Education in Colleges.* San Francisco: Jossey-Bass, 1977.

Levin, H., and R. Rumberger. "The Low Skill-Future of High Tech." *Technology Review* (August/September 1983): 18-21.

McCabe, R. H. *Why Miami-Dade Community College is Reforming the Educational Program.* Miami, Fla.: Miami-Dade Community College, 1981.

McCabe, R. H. and S. B. Skidmore. "Miami-Dade Results Justify Reforms." *Community and Junior College Journal* 54, no. 8 (September 1983): 26-29.

Parnell, D. "Five Critical Issues." *Community and Junior College Journal* 54, no.8 (May 1984a): 40-41.

_____. "Opportunity with Excellence: Vision of the Future." Interview by Dale F. Campbell and Robert M. Stivender, 13 June 1984b. Tape recording, American Association of Community and Junior Colleges, Washington, D.C.

Peters, T. J., and R. H. Waterman, Jr. *In Search of Excellence: Lessons from America's Best-Run Companies.* New York: Harper and Row, 1982.

Porter, R. C. *Cooperative Education: A Social Contract for Economic Renewal.* Boston: National Commission for Cooperative Education, n.d.

Rippey, D. T., and D. F. Campbell. "General Education in Occupational Programs." *Journal of Studies in Technical Careers* 4, no.2 (Spring 1982): 153-160.

Roueche, J. E. "Leadership for Excellence." Paper presented at the Presidents' Leadership Institute, Catawba Valley Technical College, Hickory, North Carolina, March 1984a.

_____. "Between a Rock and a Hard Place." *Community and Junior College Journal* 54, no. 7 (April 1984b): 21-24.

Roueche J. E., G. A. Baker, III, and S. D. Roueche. *College Responses to Low-Achieving Students: A National Study.* Orlando, Fla. HBJ-Media Systems, 1984c.

Salisbury, A. L. "Cooperative Education in Community Colleges." In *50 Views of Cooperative Education,* ed. D. C. Hunt 4th ed. Detroit, MI: Mid West Center for Cooperative Education, 1978: 62-64.

Williams, D. "Leaders as Teachers." In *The Princeton Papers.* Ontario, Canada: Northern Telecom, 1983: 20-21.

Zanker, A. "Why Europe Lags in Creating More Jobs." *U.S. News & World Report* 97, no. 2 (July 9, 1984): 75.

Chapter 4

HUMAN RESOURCE DEVELOPMENT

Researcher,
James O. Hammons
Professor and Coordinator
Higher Education
University of Arkansas
Fayetteville, Arkansas

Practitioner,
James L. Hudgins
President
Sumter Area Technical College
Sumter, South Carolina

Principal Resource Persons Reviewed in this Chapter

Rationale

There is nothing more important to institutions and to the future than their staff. The effectiveness in selecting people, placing them in the job, orienting them, developing them, utilizing them, and finally appraising and rewarding their performance is the key to our future—even as it has determined our past. The development of human resources must be as continuous and as well planned as the development of programs. Achieving excellence will come only if colleges institutionalize human resource development programs and accompany these with necessary organizational development. This will occur only through the strong leadership of the president and active support by managers throughout the institution.

James O. Hammons

I believed a leader could operate successfully as a kind of advisor to his organization. I thought I could avoid being a 'boss.' Unconsciously, I suspect, I hoped to duck the unpleasant necessity of making difficult decisions . . . I thought that maybe I could operate so that everyone would like me—that 'good human relations' would eliminate all discord and disagreement.

I could not have been more wrong. It took a couple of years, but I finally began to realize that a leader cannot avoid the exercise of authority any more than he can avoid the responsibility for what happens to his organization.

James L. Hudgins quoting
Douglas McGregor

Perhaps no job in business and industry is more important than that of the first-line supervisor-manager. This person is a buffer, mediator, communicator, jack-of-all-trades; and, by and large, one who must master all of these skills. Human resource development of any organization keys upon the intuitiveness of the midlevel manager. This precariously positioned individual must match the needs and aspirations of the community college instructor with the goals and objectives of the institution.

Management is not about making things and selling things, it's about people . . . Management of people is what counts . . . Don't look for excuses when the product fails, look in the mirror . . . Big organizations are dumb, keep it (management) simple.

W. Wayne Scott

OBJECTIVES

An understanding of this chapter should enable the reader to do the following:
1. Conceptualize the interdependence of faculty evaluation, motivation, and development. Faculty do not involve themselves with things with which they are not familiar and for which they are not rewarded.
2. Enhance the mid-manager's capacity to motivate a community college instructor.
3. Initiate the process of faculty evaluation-motivation-development.

INTRODUCTION

Survival of the community college, in an age when information is the most expensive resource, depends on effective and efficient use of faculty and staff. A dynamic human resource development program is paramount. Creative thinking and innovative commitments by college administration will provide solutions to keeping personnel in a state-of-the-art readiness.

Tomorrow's community college managers will face extremely complex situations. Decisions will be made under circumstances where the complex data necessary for traditional decision-making process will be unavailable, inadequate or too costly to gather quickly. Agor's writings (1983) indicate that intuitive personnel development will provide managers with an advantage in analyzing complex issues. When all faculty and staff maintain an effective, pertinent evaluation-motivation-development process, the decision making within the organization is simple and efficient.

Characteristics indicating needed human resource development are described in the expressed predicament: "The human problems generated by institutional uncertainty are numerous. On many campuses the inhabitants feel lonely, isolated, hostile, competitive, insecure and anxious. They often feel powerless to change the establishment or to control their own lives. Institutions, by and large, offer few opportunities for individuals to shape themselves and their environments. Campuses offer little encouragement for simultaneously learning to comprehend, to feel and to create or to take risks and to behave with honesty . . . " (Hammons 1984).

The balance sheet of a college does not itemize the most valuable assets. In fact, this resource of human effectiveness and vitality is not measured in dollars and has never been accurately evaluated. DeHart (1982) indicates that community college vitality will be gained by applying better ways to evaluate this resource and to preserve and enhance it. Accurate and meaningful programs of faculty evaluation are prerequisite to human resource development.

A compelling rationalization for faculty/staff development is the need to articulate college training programs with business and industry training programs. Castro (1984) stated, "Higher education is preoccupied with the business world—its notions of reality, accountability and style. What is the business world really like and what lessons does it have for the success of educational practice?"

Effective faculty/staff programs of evaluation and development will identify specific industry needs. Compromising situations exist in which subjects and courses are offered not because students wanted or needed them but because an essentially autonomous group of academic professionals could and would teach nothing else. To maintain or increase student enrollment, colleges directed faculty to drop unpalatable offerings and offer undemanding courses. Rudolph (1984) points out that the results confirmed the inadequate management of faculty-staff development programs and emphasized the authority of faculty and students. The curriculum and its application to business and industry was robbed of any credibility.

The "burn out" of instructors provides additional justification of human resource development. The sense of purpose that compels beginning eager instructors becomes vague and distant. No longer does a clear purpose exist to build upon much less provide a model for others.

Business and industry needs must be used as an approach to faculty retraining. Unless colleges can develop a systematic development program, the claim can no longer be made to produce direct benefits for student and industry. Entrenched career programs dependent on a core of faculty with outdated teaching skills make career education a cruel irony in community colleges. Two basic trends are evident in human resource development. One trend is to add new faculty to serve new programs and a new student clientele. This is more convenient than overcoming the change resistance from continuing faculty. The second trend is to "selectively" allocate funds from declining programs to high demand programs. This redistribution of resources would replace faculty as programs changed. "Both trends fail to address the issue of institutional adjustment to shifting or declining resources in community colleges through retraining of faculty" (Alfred and Nash 1983).

Researcher

Institutional renewal within community colleges should begin with an effective faculty development process. The product of the institution (education of the student) is totally dependent on the faculty and their creative use of all available resources. Development of the faculty is stressed by both internal and external forces.

Should community college education emulate business and industry training? Faculty and administration view business and industry as being what academia is not—self-confident, up-to-date, competitive, well coordinated, regulated by close accountability and compatible with mass production technology. "We are impressed with the power associated with being business-like" (Castro 1984).

How much of an association should community colleges have with business and industry? Will faculty be business and industry trained in addition to being academically trained? Business and industry personnel development leaders will be recognized as educators as they provide full-scale training programs.

Dunn (1983) recognizes that America's business and industry are steadily improving the educational preparation of personnel trainers. As of August 1983, over 100 formal academic programs exist for human resource development personnel in the United States, with at least 40 at the master's and doctoral levels. As these human resource development leaders become credentialed as educators, the lines will be further blurred; and it will be easier for colleges to create linkages.

The perception of developmental needs by an individual faculty is affected by their current performance. Individual performance is indicated by the faculty's activities resulting in either a positive or negative effect on the attainment of individual and organizational goals and objectives. Hammons (1984) recognizes five factors that determine individual performance:

1. *Ability*
   - Current Capacity to Perform

- Capability
- Includes:
  — Intellectual factors (verbal, numerical, and special skills)
  — manual factors
  — personality traits
  WHAT A PERSON *CAN* DO
2. *Motivation*
   - That something that comes from within that causes you to use your capacity
   - Willingness to perform
   - There are numerous motivators
   WHAT A PERSON *WILL* DO
3. *Climate* - A set of characteristics that describe an organization's internal environment and that:
   — are relatively enduring
   — distinguish that organization from others
   — are clearly perceived by members of the organization
   — serve as a basis for interpreting each situation/happening
   — influence the behavior of people in the organization
   — result from the way the members of the organization (especially those in top management) deal with its behavior (i.e., policies, procedures), its members, and its environment.
4. *Opportunity* - Factors beyond employee's direct control that influence whether or not they have the *chance* to perform.
5. *Environment* - Forces external to an organization that have the potential for influencing the organization.

Performance of personnel within an institution is influenced by these stated performance factors. Administration must recognize these factors and utilize them in a developmental process. Evaluation of faculty performance has been transformed in several vital areas in recent years and is still changing. The changes reflect administrative and professional realization that evaluation is more than a means for discipline measures or merit pay. The best results are for professional and institutional development. The human resource development process is much more effective by initiating Hammons' (1984) performance appraisal system:

1. Determine the purposes of the organization
   A. Mission
   B. Long-term goals (3-5 years)
   C. Short-range objectives (1 year)
2. Determine the role(s) of the staff. What is each person to do?
3. Establish a committee
   A. Clarity of charge and role are crucial
   B. Representative membership with high credibility is essential.
   C. Determine committee process (chairperson, secretary, minutes, policies, etc.)

D.	Task	Who is responsible	Due date	Resources needed

4. Prepare the committee
   A. Determine staff opinion regarding present appraisal system and appraisal in general
   B. Contact other institutions believed to have good systems

C. Conduct literature review
5. Define the *purposes* of the system
6. Determine possible *areas* and *criteria* (what is to be measured)
7. Establish proposed *standards* (achievement level) to be used and *evidence* (documentation) needed
8. Determine process to be used in implementing the system
   A. Who evaluates (Superior(s) of person appraised, peers, subordinates, persons outside immediate work environment, appraisee (self-evaluation))
   B. When to evaluate (frequency—annually, etc.)
   C. How to collect data (forms, dates, etc.)
   D. Weighing (how much value to what?)
9. Develop grievance procedure
10. Disseminate proposed plan and solicit suggestions
11. Review recommendations and revise plan
12. Issue plan and announce strategy for subsequently reviewing and modifying plan
    A. After first complete cycle
    B. Periodically thereafter
13. Train appropriate personnel in implementation

Keep all constituencies informed during planning stages

Institutional commitment is required to allow faculty to keep up with their discipline in new materials and methodology developments. Just to keep up, the faculty must be allowed considerable amounts of time to collect, format and present information via the new technologies. Time must be allowed for the developmental tasks of diagnosing student needs and prescribing individual courses of study.

The characteristics within an instructional organization can become an issue to human resource development. Anxiety, stress and alienation among midlevel managers and administration results in political grouping, harmful competition and noncooperation among the various departments. An organization that has become politicized is stale and nonproductive. Elsner (1981) observed that the greatest deterrent to politicization is to have programs allowing management to develop a clear sense of their own competencies and skills.

Effective staff developement will help to insure vitality in the college. Faculty and staff are to be encouraged to work consciously for the enhancement of personal vitality as a fundamental goal. Vitality is characterized by growth in skills and capabilities, by purpose and direction and by accomplishment (DeHart 1982). Effective staff development results in individuals who are self-motivated to get the most out of competencies and skills and to become successful within the organization.

Presidential Practitioner

The straight-forward philosophy of management expressed by Peters and Waterman (1982) places the action at the level of the people who are doing the work. In a community college the action workers are the instructors. Instructors provide the service required by the public in using the community college to meet their individual goals and objectives. A well-managed instructor is engaged in a continuous process of evaluation, motivation and development. The three phases of the process are inseparable. Each phase is linked together. Each phase requires external examination from a manager and internal examination from the instructor. The key to this active process comes from the management. A case study for this active process is Sumter Technical Institute (Hudgins 1984).

Leaders tend to color an organization with their characteristics. Activeness and intrusiveness from management create a positive climate for continuous development (Hammons 1984). Some characteristics of this climate include:

- An Environment of Trust
- Permission to Fail (Tight-loose)
- Expectations of Excellence
- Goal Orientation
- Collaborative Relationships
- Personal Goals Match College Goals
- Recognition of Realities
- Communications

With these eight characteristics, again the emphasis is on keeping it simple and involving the people. The effective and continuous management process of evaluation, motivation and development is further explained with the "Eight Rules" on "To Be The Best" (Hudgins 1984):

1. *Bias for Action*
2. *Stay Close to the Customer*
3. *Simple Form-Lean Staff*
4. *Hands On-Value Driven*
5. *Autonomy and Entrepreneurship*
6. *Productivity Through People*
7. *Stick to the Knitting*
8. *Simultaneous Loose-Tight Properties* (Peters & Waterman 1982).

Colleges that are confused as to how to develop their personnel resources have no difficulty in offering a course of study equally confusing to the student. Evaluation of curricula and faculty is a key component of faculty development. Predevelopment evaluation and postdevelopment evaluations are both necessary for total institutional progress. In the informational age of the 1980s, evaluation of faculty has taken on new meaning and importance. Who makes the decisions for evaluating and rewarding developmental accomplishments? If all faculty were to choose to participate in a development process and all expected to receive remuneration and promotion as rewards, the organization would experience suicide.

The evaluation process of faculty performance is the most difficult component of the total evaluation-motivation-developmental process. Speak of evaluation to faculty, and fear becomes the dominant motivator. Fear is an urgent taskmaster. Seventy-two percent of the people in the world participate in activities because they are afraid not to (Scott 1984). The major problem of fear as a motivator is the manner in which people interact. Fear creates anxieties that must be vented. Anxiety results in inner conflicts with concepts of security, trust, self-esteem and value judgment. The most effective way to evaluate people is to stimulate a recognition of needs. Individuals are hesitant to acknowledge their needs. Scott (1984) gives two reasons as to why people won't tell their needs:

1. they don't know, and
2. they are afraid of their own judgment.

"To the degree you can reduce judgment to zero, you can motivate people."

Accurate evaluation and assessment of the instructor/curriculum activities reveal the institutional and personal needs, and the available resources. The administrative support of faculty/staff development is crucial. Once the commitment from the top is established, an assessment process should begin. Recognition of these existing activities will often reveal a base for building a formal program. Accomplishing institutional and individual needs assessments is the most important assignment facing the staff developer. The questionnaire and the personal interview are the two most popular methods for such assessment. Personal interviews take time but often build support. Questionnaires reach larger numbers and bring uniformity to the process.

Staff and organizational development is a synergistic partnership of the total institution. A relationship exists between climate, ability and motivation that must be assessed, analyzed and utilized. This change model has been effectively applied to a continuous faculty/staff development at Sumter Area Technical College.

Once a commitment to a formal staff development has been made by the administration, staff and total institution, a philosophy for staff development should evolve. To provide a focus, the members of the institution who are to be served should develop and approve this philosophy. It will deal with need and importance as well as basic guiding principles. Putting the philosophy into action should be the responsibility of a staff development coordinator. A coordinator of staff development, assisted by an institutional wide representative committee, will maintain focus of activities.

A Case Study for Human Resource Development

At Sumter Area Technical College, the evaluation-motivation-development process is an accepted way of life. When James L. Hudgins took the helm in May, 1978 as the institution's second president, the attitude for organizational development was right and the process became a realization. Hudgins began the development process by applying the action definition used by Jim Hammons in the book *Organization Development: Change Strategies.* "Organizational Development represents change that is planned, is pursued in a systematic fashion, is expected to occur over a long period, is systems oriented, is managed, is based on participation and involvement by those concerned, takes into account both data and experience, emphasizes goal setting and planning, is implemented with a contingency approach, and focuses on intact work teams."

Hudgins began the developmental process at Sumter by the formation of major phases for change:
- Step 1 - Awareness of Need for Change
- Step 2 - Diagnosis
- Step 3 - Action Plans, Strategies & Techniques
- Step 4 - Monitoring, Evaluating & Stabilizing

With the assistance of John McKay, Vice-President for Educational Affairs, a process of analysis of the existing conditions began. McKay developed a rationale for introducing a significant change strategy. The awareness of need for change became apparent to the more creative members of the faculty and staff.

The technique used by Hudgins in diagnosing the need for change was direct and effective, containing all the essential elements:

- Sincere - intended to utilize results
- Broad-Based - involved all elements of organization
- Diagnostic - sought to identify real problems

The diagnosis took place in two phases:

1. Survey conducted in May of 1978 which asked three questions:
   a. Identify five most important functions of the president
   b. Identify five greatest problems confronting Sumter Area Technical College
   c. Identify the five most important priorities for Sumter Area Technical College
2. A planning process initiated during the year contained a SWOT's analysis:
   Strengths
   Weaknesses
   Opportunities
   Threats

In compliance with his commitment to a continual development process, Hudgins repeated the survey in 1983.

The survey results became the foundation for the continuing developmental process. The results were utilized to introduce immediate and long-range action plans. Immediate action was indicated to be structural changes and personnel changes. The survey specifically pointed out personnel changes in the areas of transfers, recruitment and termination. Long-range changes focused on specific issues including staff development, evaluation, student recruitment and marketing and competency-based education. In meeting the staff development needs, Hudgins used the model previously referenced in this writing. With the assistance of Dianne Brandstadter, Hudgins developed Sumter's Action Plan for Faculty and Staff Development.

The final step in this organizational development process was to initiate a continual process of faculty and program evaluation. Hudgins experienced difficulties common to higher education—what should the outcomes of evaluation be and how should these outcomes be measured? Nevertheless, efforts continued to be made and results realized at Sumter. Measurable results were obtained from critical areas such as enrollment increases, student demographic changes, changes in program offerings, changes in revenue sources, increase in calibre of faculty and staff and improvement in physical facilities.

The leadership provided by Hudgins was paramount in the organizational development process at Sumter Area Technical College. Hudgins' philosophy is that the president should use his/her leadership skills to make Organizational Development possible by (1) creating a climate for change, and (2) establishing a structure for change. This philosophy has led Sumter Area Technical College to the exemplary model for Human Resource Development.

Models of Human Resource Development

The faculty seminar has been used in some situations as an effective means to faculty/staff development. Schwoebel (1984) points out the Faculty Seminar at Temple University as an ad hoc, self-selected, ongoing group. The purpose of this seminar is a self-analysis of instructional problems. In the initial meetings for planning of development policies, this group discovered that a common understanding of the nature and definition of higher education did not exist. Each faculty member perceived the purpose of the total institution to be characteristic of their own philosophy.

The proceedings toward a faculty/staff development program became effective only after a common understanding of objectives and philosophy was reached. The seminar studied various issues relating to transition from an industrial society to a service economy. Conclusions resulted in the construction of a program that would deal specifically with the educational needs of a typically service economy population. This seminar's efforts resulted in the Gateway Program. The purpose of the Gateway Program was to demonstrate that individuals with a variety of educational backgrounds and at different points in life could communicate positively to develop a common need. The group carefully designed learning experiences that helped them to determine what they needed, what they could get, and what they could handle.

Astute institutions will establish a faculty development program that alters organizational norms and cultivates faculty development as a desirable activity. Chait and Gueths (1981) suggest specific design criteria for a model program of faculty development.

An effective model for faculty/staff development could avoid remedial topics such as "teaching teachers how to teach." A survey of twenty-four colleges and universities revealed that ninety percent of the faculty judged themselves to be "above average" or "superior teachers." Instruction is most likely to be improved when development programs are concerned with pertinent topics related to what is needed in the curriculum.

First, the program should focus on professional roles and activities rather than on individual, program or organizational needs. Developmental activities that are consonant with the image of an accomplished instructor and convey a measure of prestige should be promoted. Second, the program should have a developmental approach and a constructive rationale rather than a remedial purpose. Correctly aimed faculty/staff development programs are the third design. The orientation should be to encourage and reward participants so that institutional norms are changed and individuals eventually elect to participate for fear of peer pressure.

The fourth design is that developmental programs should be faculty centered and not administratively directed. A faculty review board should accept proposals and reward funding for individual development programs. This reward process would be faculty controlled and accepted. Fifth, the program should be structured institutional-wide and not by department. A cross-departmental program would have the advantage in that resources can be shifted to fund the departments with the most demanding development needs. Sixth, the rewards for faculty development should be both economic and noneconomic resulting in fulfilling individual desires and promoting individuals to maintain the status quo. Conversely, where the perceived risks of innovation are few and the potential payoffs are many, individuals will be disposed more favorable to change. The faculty development program should enable prospective participants to choose from the widest range of activities. The reward structure should permit successful participants to choose from the widest possible array of intrinsic and extrinsic payoffs.

The creative use of a human resource development model is continguent on the application of certain generalizations (Hudgins 1984):

- finding an intelligent point of coordination for these activities.
- realizing that the best faculty development programs are probably highly decentralized, and even undermanaged, as far as the intrusion of administration is concerned.

- knowing that monetary incentives and release time deliver better results than grand designs at the central office.
- recognizing that as in management development, external forces or even personal crisis have more to do with the successful initiation of change than the best designed plans.
- acknowledging peer or colleague influence as a major component of good faculty development programs.
- concluding that the best faculty development programs appear to be jointly designed by administration and faculty and combined with facilitative support (not always money) from the administration.
- realizing that most good faculty development programs are tied to missions of the institution, but also are good solo flights for individual initiative.

IMPLICATIONS

An effective and efficient process of evaluation-motivation-development offers many intriguing results. Intriguing, in that innovative and sometimes irrational ideas can offer potential profits that will turn a stale organization into an energetic and dynamic force. Community colleges will be looked toward in the future to serve as the trendsetter in continuity of learning. When proper development occurs, the community colleges would fit the description offered by Parnell (1984), ". . . if there is one word that really describes the community, technical and junior colleges of this country, it would be the word 'opportunity.' I would . . . choose to use the word 'access' because it is a little more descriptive than even the word 'opportunity.' Access to higher education, that's one of the roles of the community college." The premier implication of human resource development is to provide access to the opportunity.

Initially the advantages of human resource development would be to the individual. Ideally, development would result in a change of attitude and a change of behavior. Positive attitude and behavior changes of the individual would simultaneously benefit the total institution. Built into the developmental process would be a rewards system for an individual's improved performance; including merit pay, sizable raises and promotions.

Monetary benefits would be only a part of the implications of development. With less direct financial resources involved, individuals could gain advantages more gratifying, in some situations, than a pay raise. Development reward could be a teaching assistant, additional laboratory equipment, increased supplies and materials budget, a teaching load reduction, increased travel funds, and possibly a sabbatical.

Invaluable to many individuals are those rewards which offer no monetary gains. Everyone appreciates recognition. After completing a developmental process, the individual could be recognized by being offered opportunities to give advice, influence decisions and serve on key committees. These individuals could have a more compact schedule, more advanced courses, exposure in professional publications. Recognition with a certificate, medal or plaque. These individuals could be honored with an opportunity to a luncheon with the dean, president or board of trustees. Contrarily, to the individual the most desirable reward may be to be exempt from certain meetings and committees.

Professionals most often gain satisfaction from intrinsic rewards, the satisfaction of a job well done. Developmental processes will result in an increase of professional status and respect from colleagues. Much worth can be gained from professional status and peer recognition.

Community colleges can only improve in the service of educating the public by developing the process of evaluation-motivation-development. Retraining the faculty will balance the student interests and industry needs with faculty instructional proficiency. Revitalized faculty will have the insight needed to improve institutional performance in relation to changing economic conditions, shifting labor market needs and rapid advances in technology.

Development of systematic approaches to faculty retraining predicated to business and industry will improve institutional responsiveness to the following: 1) fluctuations in industry needs for trained manpower and 2) changing conditions governing the supply of faculty in emerging high demand career fields such as business, allied health and the engineering sciences (Alfred 1983). Continual employment of the evaluation-motivation-development process will gain for the community college vauable information about the quality of institutional resources and products. The process will reveal an open analysis of such vital components of the organizational operation as the teaching faculty, curriculum organization, institutional strategies, equipment inventories, program planning and evaluation processes, academic support services and student outcomes. Institutional advantages will be gained from acknowledging program deficiencies. The evaluation-motivation-development process will initiate corrective actions to implement the improvement of instructional performance and preparation of students for business and industry.

Profits from a persistant human resource developmental process will fulfill the premier objective of effectively and efficiently employing the institutional means to provide access to an opportunity for excellence in continual learning.

CONCLUSION

Recommendations to Division/Department Chairpersons

The process of faculty development is most effective when administered in three phases: 1) evaluation, 2) motivation, and 3) development. Based on the references cited in this writing, the effective continual process of evaluation-motivation-development is contingent on the application of several pertinent steps.

Evaluation Steps:
- Develop an awareness of a need to change.
- Create a non-threatening climate for change.
- Assist the faculty in establishing specific standards of instructional and program performance.
- Lead the individual faculty members in an analysis process to determine differences in performance and the established standard.
- Identify the specific needs in meeting the established standards.

Motivation Steps:
- At all times maintain a positive relationship with the faculty.
- Establish a rewards system that will compensate the efforts required to complete the developmental task.
- Assure the faculty that the rewards system is an indispensable component of the developmental process.
- Allow faculty the flexibility to select developmental processes that will

develop them as a person and not just improve their function to the institution.

Development Steps:
- Provide the time and appropriate resources for faculty development.
- Allow the faculty the flexibility to participate in developmental activities that will be personally fulfilling.
- Organize the rewards system so that the appropriate means of recognition for developmental efforts will be administered.
- Structure the operation of the division/department so that the gained development will become a real part of the operation.

Reviewer for this Chapter

John T. German
Associate Dean of the College
Wilkes Community College
Wilkesboro, North Carolina

REFERENCES

Agor, W. H. "Tomorrow's Intuitive Leaders." *The Futurist* 17, no. 4 (August 1983): 49-53.

Alfred, R. L. "Faculty Retraining: A Strategic Response to Changing Resources and Technology." *Community College Review* 11, No. 2 (Fall 1983): 3-8.

Castro, B. "Outside the Ivory Tower: Learning About Education at the Workplace." *Change* 16, no. 4 (May/June 1984): 35-41.

Chait, R. P., and J. Gueths. "Proposing a Framework for Faculty Development." *Change* 13, no. 4 (May/June 1981): 30-33.

DeHart, R. A. "Thank God it's Monday." *Community and Junior College Journal* 52, no.6. (March 1982): 12-15.

Dunn, S. L. "The Changing University: Survival in the Information Society." *The Futurist* 17, no. 4, (August 1983): 55-60.

Elsner, P. A. "Management as a Creative Human Resource." *Community and Junior College Journal* 52, no. 5 (August 1983): 55-60.

Hammons, J. O. "Human Resource Development." Paper presented at the Presidents' Leadership Institute, Technical College of Alamance, Haw River, North Carolina, February 1984.

Hudgins, J. L. "Human Resource Development." Paper presented at the Presidents' Leadership Institute, Technical College of Alamance, Haw River, North Carolina, February 1984.

Parnell, D. "Opportunity with Excellence: Vision of the Future." Interview by Dale F. Campbell and Robert M. Stivender, 13 June 1984. Tape recording, American Association of Community and Junior Colleges, Washington, D.C.

Peters, T. J., and R. H. Waterman, Jr. *In Search of Excellence*. New York: Harper and Row, 1982.

Rudolph, F. "The Power of Professors - The Impact of Specialization and Professionalization on the Curriculum." *Change* 16, no. 4 (May/June 1984): 12-17.

Schwoebel, R., and N. R. Bartel. "Revitalizing the Faculty." *Change* 14, no.8 (November/December 1982): 22-23.

Scott, W. W. "Human Resource Development." Paper presented at the Presidents' Leadership Institute, Technical College of Alamance, Haw River, North Carolina, February 12-14, 1984.

Scott, W. W., and J. T. Miller. *Every Supervisor a Winner*. Clarkston, Georgia: Janco Publishers, 1979.

Seldin, P. "Faculty Evaluation." *Change* 16, no. 3 (April 1984): 28-33.

Chapter 5

COMPUTERS AND TELECOMMUNICATIONS

Researcher,
Louis W. Bender
Professor of Higher Education
Florida State University
Tallahassee, Florida

Practitioner,
Carl Christian Andersen
President
Dyersburg State Community College
Dyersburg, Tennessee

Principal Resource Persons Reviewed in this Chapter

RATIONALE

Small two year colleges represent a strategic element in the nation's post-secondary educational system. These institutions are often the only resource available for educational access, occupational preparation, upgrading or retraining. The use of new technology for instructional and administrative applications in such institutions is critical if they are to fulfill their mission and full potential.

Louis W. Bender and
Lora P. Conrad

The involvement and encouragement of the college president is necessary for a smooth transition into using administrative tools such as MIS and data base management. Managers of computer departments must be fully aware of the context of the professional educational institution.

Carl Christian Andersen

Graphic communications will replace paper for storage and communication of information. Electronic mail, interactive disc, and teleconferencing will replace the memo.

William L. Ballenger

Educational leaders are facing a technological revolution which impacts every area of the institution and dictates new strategies for planning and decision making. This rapid technological change will also bring to administrators invaluable resources and an incredible range of options to use as they develop new administrative skills. Institutional leaders will be required to sort through, target and implement change strategies to support both administrative functions and instructional activities. The response of community colleges to these needs will set the future course. Dunn (1983) states "exciting days are ahead for those institutions that can make the transition and realize the unlimited potential of the information society."

The rise of the community college movement was directly related to their ability and willingness to be people's colleges, linked to local industry and providing practical skill training or general education parallel to the first two years of a four-year degree. Their adaptive flexibility and spontaneous reaction to community needs make community colleges "the most important educational contribution of the mid-20th century" (McCabe 1981). But will the people's colleges show this same adaptive strategy in accepting and integrating the latest technology?

OBJECTIVES

The opportunities and issues which the emerging technologies bring to the community college require some examination. How can technology be used to solve the educational administrator's dilemma of translating a profusion of data into useful management information to assist in decision making? Specifically this chapter will:

1. Provide an overview of computer and telecommunication technologies and their impact on post-secondary institutions.
2. Enhance understanding of new management tools and organizational structures to improve institutional administration and decision-making.
3. Examine ways to enhance the capacity of institutional leaders in an attempt to utilize appropriate forms of technology to improve services to their communities.

INTRODUCTION

Computers are a leading technology in what John Naisbitt (1984) has described as the information society. They are touted as the answer to both the manager's and the educator's dreams. College administration must develop practical skills in decision making, must be actively involved in assessing and selecting appropriate management and instructional tools, and must plan and implement technologies which will relate to the mission of the college.

Educators, already at work in the knowledge business, should look to technology and telecommunications as an effective means of expanding and improving services. The evolution into the information age signals significant changes in the issues and decisions facing community college leaders who must respond to insure that colleges manipulate and direct use of technology to their and the learners' benefit. Administrators, faculty and students need new strategies to adapt to these issues and their societal and economic impact. Skills not now possessed will be needed to manage, teach or learn with the new technologies.

Two areas in the college which likely will be early targets for experiments in using technology are administrative/financial services and instruction. Innovative activities incorporating computer and telecommunications technologies can have immediate impact on the total institution. For example, some of the issues faced by personnel involved in implementing these initiatives are a part of any change process: long-range planning, identifying key personnel, specifying coordination and management responsibility, allocating resources, and disseminating information. Other issues are specific to the activity and department. In examining implementation of technological innovation in an administrative or instructional setting one sees some very different requirements. There would be different user groups with different needs for each system. The target for administrative computing, for instance, would be business office personnel or top-level administrators; users of instructional technology would be students and faculty.

Specific software and hardware decisions would be based on different criteria. Support of instruction is a priority in institutional planning and activity. The administrative data processing function is a support unit for the systems and personnel needed for instruction. Thus, the examination of the impact of technology on a college must be examined from those two perspectives.

First, this chapter will examine the adaptive flexibility needed by colleges to effectively integrate administrative data processing systems. Secondly, the chapter will move beyond the administrative uses of computers to examine the implications of computer and telecommunications technologies for instruction. Colleges using instructional technologies bring to adult learners new, exciting and flexible learning opportunities. The impact of these emerging technologies will be felt campus wide.

Researcher-Computers and Information Systems

Where are the institutions within the higher educational network with regard to their degree of automation by computer systems? Lou Bender and Lora Conrad sought to measure the impact and status of the computer in the two-year college via a 1983 study which utilized both survey and case study methodology. The survey was national in scope and involved almost 300 small two-year institutions. Of the 60% of institutions responding to the survey, 80% had some type of computer system and were able to provide useful information for analytical purposes. The case study involved five selected institutions which were subjected to close examination of their computer and computing function.

Results of the Study:

Planning - the need for well developed, long range planning prior to the procurement and implementation of computer and information systems was identified; however, in practice, the majority of institutions failed to execute a proper planning phase prior to the purchase of a system.

Governance and Administration - Although the placement and role definitions of computer services staff members vary considerably within the institutions, most were considered to be administrative in nature. Computer services staffs were typically small in numbers with the head of computing spending the majority of time in other roles within the institution.

Hardware and Software - Among the preponderance of IBM and DEC equipment found within the institutions surveyed, the batch processing mode was still being utilized in most cases. Software was "home grown" for the most part, originating within the institution or within a regional or state software sharing network. Software designed around a data base concept was practically non-existent.

Administrative Information Systems - Of the institutions surveyed, almost two-thirds were using their computer systems for administrative purposes, with the remainder utilizing systems for instruction. The majority of administrative uses focused on student related information systems and financial support information systems. Few of these operated in an interactive (on-line/real-time) mode or were integrated module to module.

Instructional Applications - Respondent instructional software applications included data processing instruction, computer literacy instruction, computer assisted instruction (student driven), computer managed instruction (instructor driven), and word processing instruction.

Costs - Although the resulting cost data was very general in nature, the average annual computing budget for institutions of this size ranged from $60,000-$100,000. Half of this budget amount was for personnel, with the other portion going for computer related expenses.

People - The successful interaction and communication between computer services personnel and user personnel was identified as a critical issue among the responding institutions. Staff turnover was also cited as a serious problem which effected the continuity of the computing function within the institution.

It appears as a result of this study, that the small two-year institutions have made a beginning with regard to computer automation but have a long way to go. As institutions evolve into the newer computer technologies, they should take into consideration policy implications, hardware and software implications, personnel implications, and organizational implications. With the rapid technological advancement being experienced today, together with lower hardware costs and improved software, there should be quite an advance among this level of institution in the not so distant future.

Microcomputers - Current Status of Usage

Bender and Conrad (1984b) continued their research with another national study which measured the status levels of microcomputer users in small two-year colleges.

> Computers are no longer a luxury for a college of any size but rather a basic necessity—as basic a tool for college survival as the telephone. Using computers effectively in the college environment and coping with computer literate students require a computer literate faculty, staff, and administration with access to adequate hardware and software, as well as a systematic flexible action plan.

Bender and Conrad divided their survey results into three categories of user sophistication:

1. Fledgling - Those users who are relatively inexperienced and rely on a significant amount of external assistance.
2. Apprentice - Those users who are currently growing and beginning to master their systems. They exhibit a high degree of dedication to the task but lack the experience to be proficient.
3. Sophisticate - Those users who have mastered their systems and readily integrate their computer skills into the management and operation of their institution.

The responses indicated that there are many small colleges in the fledgling category, a sizeable group in the apprentice category and very few qualified as sophisticates. Several reasons are cited for the distribution resulting in this manner:

- lack of a systematic development plan
- absence of a proper needs assessment prior to purchase
- absence of a total, orderly institutional perspective on microcomputing
- lack of proper hardware procurement policies

What are the implications of this study for institutional leaders? First of all, we must realize the potential impact of microcomputing on every individual within the institution. The need and desire for the information and data that can be provided and manipulated in an automatic fashion pervades or soon will pervade each department of the college. In order to be able to keep the pace with a department utilizing microcomputer technology, non-participating departments will have to fall in line. Additionally, the micro systems will have a terrific impact upon the ability of departments to exchange data through electronic media as opposed to a paper transfer. A non-participative department would lose the ability to have this data exchange through non-compatability. A specific listing of steps that leaders should consider in this regard are below:

- insure that needs are properly identified
- identify software first
- select hardware
- seek technical assistance (avoid excessive dependence on vendors)
- appoint a competent head of computing
- formulate a computer advisory committee
- conduct computer literacy training for all staff members
- do advanced planning and establish definite computer policies

Small colleges are well on the way to automation of certain functions through the use of microcomputers. If the proper approach is taken to this conversion, institutions will realize the true benefit of the available technology today.

Deciding on Computer Systems

One of the most challenging and confusing tasks facing modern day managers in education is that of decision making about computers. The more one reads and does research on the subject, the more confusing it becomes. Computer technology is changing so rapidly that accepted computer "truths" which have been around for more than six months are frequently no longer valid. Thus managers find themselves searching for a trend or consistent pattern, but always accepting change as the norm.

Many institutions today are utilizing advisory committees to guide and assist in the selection and administration of computers and computer policy. The first task of any such group is to thoroughly identify and prioritize the needs of the institution in the computer area. This may include management information system software, office automation software, and instructional improvement with microcomputers (Andersen 1984). Once the needs assessment is completed, the process logically evolves into specific selection processes. Institutions are faced with the selection of a variety of levels of computer systems, i.e., microcomputers, mini-computers and mainframe computers. The selection criteria and implications discussed in this section relate to all three, although for micros it is generally on a smaller scale.

In addition to advisory committees, many institutions have chosen to utilize a computer consultant as they go about the needs assessment and software/hardware selection processes. This is especially true for smaller institutions where the computer expertise on-board may not be at a satisfactory level to guide the institution through the process. In this case the commissioning of a qualified consultant is certainly more cost effective than hiring a qualified person full time.

Software:

The single most important consideration with any computer acquisition is the software to be run on the computer. The old saying that "hardware needs only to be adequate to satisfactorily run the software" is a true and valid statement. Too many managers make computer decisions based on hardware, only to find that when they begin to shop for software, rarely are applications found which fully meet their computer and computing needs. Once an institutional computing needs assessment is completed, software should be placed in the forefront prior to any hardware considerations. As Lou Bender states, "Hardware planning has been extensive but when it comes to software, very little planning is done."

Software is available to institutions in several ways:

METHOD	POSITIVE IMPLICATIONS	NEGATIVE IMPLICATIONS
1. Internal development	+ Custom tailored to needs	− Expensive, lengthy process
2. Agency exchange programs	+ Relatively inexpensive	− May not suit needs − Proprietory questions
3. Purchase of vendor software	+ Tailored to particular area + Vendor training and support	− May be expensive
4. Turnkey systems (hardware, software training, support)	+ Easy to coordinate and administer + Comprehensive scope	− May be expensive − Software must match institution's needs
5. Facilities Management (Vendor provides hardware, software, personnel)	+ Preserves salary equitability + Benefits of expensive system at fixed rate	− Role definition is difficult

As discussed earlier, many systems today utilize a data base management approach toward organizing and accessing the data of the institution. This approach provides management with a powerful tool necessary for the development of a decision support system. According to Kim Cameron (1984) of the National Center for Higher Education Management Systems, "institutions will need to rely on new kinds of decision support systems that allow preferences and interests to be instantaneously aggregated and compared." The software technology is available to accomplish this, and managers should incorporate this approach into their software plans.

Most software packages purchased today require some degree of training prior to useful implementation. Training is critically important as an ingredient in the overall success or failure of an application. The operators of any application deserve adequate, relative training prior to the actual live operation of the software. It would be interesting to quantify the occurrences of "software unsuitability" which should have actually been attributed to poor or improper operator training. Training costs must also be considered. These costs are frequently an important factor and constitute a significant portion of the bottom line of a computer purchase.

Software documentation is also an important factor in the software selection process. Understandable, meaningful user and system documentation should be provided as a part of the software purchase. This not only provides users with the instructions they need, it also acts as a safeguard against the detrimental effects of staff turnover (Bender and Conrad 1984a).

Hardware:

There are several questions which one must answer regarding the selection of appropriate computer hardware for the needs of a particular institution. In order to provide realistic answers to these questions, managers must have a feel for the intended scope and magnitude of the computer function within the institution, i.e., which departments, buildings, campuses, etc., will be users of the system(s). What will the physical location(s) of the hardware be? With resolutions to these questions in hand, managers should be prepared to answer:

- How many output devices (terminals, printers, workstations) are needed to adequately disseminate the hardware resource?
- Approximately how large are the institutional data base(s) projected to be (as measured in characters or bytes)?
- What is an acceptable operator response time to a terminal request? (Usually 2-5 seconds is acceptable.)
- What types of communications are needed - micro to main computer, main computer to main computer, building to building, campus to campus, etc.?

Effective planning is crucial as one engages in the implementation of a computer system. An effective measurement "gauge" during the planning phase is the price/performance ratio of hardware to a relative performance factor. Such information is generally available for examination from the various computer vendors.

Financing options should be examined prior to the signing of a contract for a computer system. Options typically available are straight purchase, lease/purchase, or straight lease. The features of each option should be considered for each institutional situation (Bender and Conrad 1983a).

Practitioner

Carl Christian Andersen, in his capacity as president of Dyersburg State College in Dyersburg, Tennessee, guided his institution through the implementation of a complete plan for computing, which will serve his institution for years to come. The plan also served as a model for the Tennessee Community College System.

The intent of the project was to enhance the capacity of the administrative and academic functions of the institution. Andersen himself played a key role in the leadership and direction of the project, which involved planning for the entire institution. The approach of the project came from two directions; 1) to seek a solution to the administrative computing needs, and 2) to provide an academic solution which would afford state-of-the-art computing technology to the academic areas.

Andersen's first step in the process was to solicit the assistance of Lou Bender to act as a consultant for the project, providing external computer expertise. Soon thereafter, Andersen hired a competent computer services director to serve as the central figure in the computerization process. A consideration in this decision was where to place the function of the computer head within the organization. Andersen chose to have this position report directly to him. A possible problem to be encountered by other institutions in this area, according to Andersen, is that many times a computing head comes from the private sector and has a difficult time understanding the complexities and educational problems associated with the institution today. "Unless the computing head (from the private sector) has a clear orientation to the institution, there will be no way of knowing the difference between the context of his or her world and the context of the professional educational institution." Without a clear and open channel of communication between both factions, mistrust and alienation may well develop.

Anderson organized and utilized advisory committees during the course of the entire project. They were select committees chosen from personnel within the Tennessee Community College System as well as Dyersburg State personnel. As was previously mentioned, they focused on two areas: administrative computing needs and the needs of the academic community.

The actions taken as a result of this project to date have been in the form of the following items:

- Hardware selection and purchase.
- Management information system software implementation.
- Office automation.
- Instructional improvement with microcomputers.

The future planning of the Dyersburg project calls for continued automation of the instructional function featuring increased numbers of microcomputers for students, faculty and instructional labs. The administrative plans involve a totally integrated administrative function which features a microcomputer with graphics capabilities for each administrative staff member.

Organizational Impact

An examination of the evolutionary trends with regard to the organizational accommodation and adaptation of the data processing role within most institutions reveals the fact that most functions in the computer area had their beginnings within the business office. For that reason, the chief business official acted, either formally or informally, as the data processing manager. Lou Bender sums this up, "The person in charge is usually in the area where the computer started in the institution." This relates primarily to the mini/mainframe world since control of microcomputers typically resides with the individual users. An overall plan for micro control will aid the management of the entire computer resource base for the institution.

As hardware and software have become more sophisticated and comprehensive, the computer has evolved into an institution-wide resource. Therein lies a dilemma—should the business officer continue to function as the computer resource manager for the system which is shared by many departments with many different interests? According to Bender and Conrad, "Most administrators recognize the potential power that resides with the control of finances. Too few, however, realize the magnitude of the power emanating from information." Many institutions have opted in recent years to structure the data processing function with its own manager, director or vice president. The trend toward a separate position as head of computing (assuming the institution is of sufficient size for this to be possible) will most likely continue in the future. As a rule today, salaries of the computing head and associate staff members exceed those of other comparable personnel within the institution. This should level out somewhat in the future as computer trained persons increase in numbers in the job marketplace.

The computing function will have to be controlled and managed at an appropriate management level within the institution. Beyond that, the resource itself should support the informational and decisional needs of all groups within the organization.

CONCLUSION

Only through proper needs assessment, planning, selection, implementation, and management of the institution's computer resources will we as managers be able to survive in the information society. Bender emphasizes this point stating very simply that "information is power." Managers have a choice—to join the participation of the computer/information movement or to hold out and rely on conventional methodology. Those choosing the latter have only limited years of surviability before they will become totally obsolescent.

Beyond Administrative Technology

The administrative uses of computers and other information technologies represent only one area of impact on an educational institution. At least as significant for the college's future is the potential for dramatic changes in curriculum and instruction which technology offers. The opportunity to use computers as management tools has made top-level managers and business officials focus on technology in a different way. Faculty and instructional administrators also have faced the changes brought by technology. One technolgoy, television, has gained widespread acceptance and use as a teaching/learning tool both on-campus and at home. Broadcast television courses, begun in the 1930s became a staple in some regions by the 1950s. With the creation of the Public Broadcasting System in 1969, widespread networking began for development and use of high quality television series for academic credits. Early users of television and radio courses moved quickly to integrate instructional telecommunications into their institutional operations.

Expansion of the early technologies and newer developments added significantly to the potential of telecommunications in education. Broadcasting has given way to "narrowcasting," directing television signals to smaller specific audiences. This can be accomplished by newer directional and individual technologies including ITFS (Instructional Television Fixed Service), DBS (Direct Broadcast Satellite), cassettes, cable, microwave, personal computers, teletext, videodisc, fiber-optics and more. All these bring unique features to the instructional telecommunications future. Linkages of the technologies then expand the possibilities tenfold, and are already available. Video imaging and microcomputing technologies will be linked more and more as the cost declines and the applications expand. The technologies will surely force changes in our traditional educational assumptions. If not, David Butler's prediction (1982) of a student turned-on to pocket calculators and home computers and turned-off to our traditional learning systems will signal our demise.

Instructional Technology and the College Mission

College mission statements can be the most important place to incorporate the commitment to opportunity and access to education that the technologies can provide. Dale Parnell, President of the American Association of Community and junior Colleges, in a recent interview reiterated the access theme as the most important function of a community college (Parnell 1984). He cited access to economic opportunity through skill training, access to quality of life experiences such as cultural and liberal arts education, and access to opportunities for lifelong learning.

Naisbitt (1984) discusses three stages for technological innovation. First, the changes follow the path of least resistance, applied in ways that do not threaten people. This can be seen in the practices at some colleges of labelling alternative courses using television or computers as "experimental"; granting credits through continuing education only; limiting enrollment to those not seeking degrees; or excluding veterans or other financial aid students who have rigid attendance requirements. In some colleges, neither administrators nor faculty believe instructional telecommunications are here to stay. Luskin (1983) tells of faculty reaction to the "fad" of telecourses. Their position, he states, is "that we must stand firm against the intrusion of this technology into our institutions." This attitude reinforces the necessity of identifying, hiring and encouraging those committed to using technologies and bringing others along slowly by demonstrating success. We only can hope that fewer and fewer institutions and educators remain at this first stage.

Many institutions are at Naisbitt's second stage: using technology to improve what we already have. Video can bring new visual experiences into courses. History, geography, social science and humanities come alive through drama or documentary. Computers simulate expensive or dangerous training situations, or bring science experiments alive by collapsing or expanding time. Radio broadcasts or audiotape loans can give students convenience and control of instruction. Ease of use and availability must be watchwords for the education of the future.

The third stage involves new directions which grow out of the technology itself. This is just beginning with computer networking, interactive systems, learner-directed videodisc and combined technologies paving the way for significant changes in the mass-produced education of the past. Individualization can become more than rhetoric with the opportunity to develop learning activities directed by students' choices and specific to their needs. Naisbitt (1984) says we can no longer learn from the past what to plan for, but must look to the future for planning information.

The integration of technologies within our colleges can significantly increase convenient and cost-effective access for all learners. But college leaders must set the stage for this integration by defining the college mission in a way which encourages movement into educational technology and telecommunications. This will require long-range planning involving all areas of the institution. An ad hoc committee approach or a development team concept should be considered consisting of personnel from academic departments, marketing, registration, student support services and the business office. This is the same concept suggested in examining use of computer systems in administration. Long-range planning tied to the mission statement is a fundamental requirement for colleges to be adequately prepared to meet the challenges the new technologies afford in both instruction and administration.

Organizational Impact

The instructional technologies are hardware and software intensive compared with labor intensive classroom instruction. This presents an interesting dilemma for educators in assessing the impact of technology on resource management. It appears that the first requirement in using the technologies is to make the institutional commitment to allocate resources for and channel energies into a new direction. This echoes the commitment required for introducing computer and data management systems. Looking at the vast array of instructional alternatives, colleges need to assess needs of their range of learners, allocate resources to those alternatives which now and in the future offer the most promise, and begin to identify and solicit needed financial and human resources. Managers and faculty who support the changes will be critical to the success of the endeavor.

What does this mean to traditional administrators, mid-level managers, and faculty in traditional institutions? A promotion packet from the Public Broadcasting Service's Adult Learning Service states, "Hundreds of colleges and universities succeed in offering . . . television courses; a few fail. When asked what makes their efforts work, top administrators and institutions successfully using television courses say it is their *commitment* to the concept—their belief that television courses are an integral part of their curriculum" (ALS 1984).

These administrators list three keys in the process:
1. Allocate sufficient human and financial resources to successfully teach and support telecourses.
2. Integrate television courses into curriculum planning, giving them comparable status and credit to on-campus courses.
3. Plan for long-term involvement by setting goals, evaluating, and adapting to fit student needs. (ALS 1984)

Because some faculty *will* be threatened by increasing use of technologies, they will need assistance and support from academic administrators at all levels (Zigerell 1982). If the technology is to be well used, new roles for faculty must be defined and new instructional strategies adopted. Administrators must create an environment where the proper skills or incentives are available for both faculty and students. For students, individual initiative and discipline are required by "distance" learners to a larger degree than by classroom students, although Luskin (1983) makes the point that students are not "distant" from the material, only from the campus, classroom or instructor. For example, although the quality of the educational experience is usually rated very high by telecourse students, they also may need different skills to function fully as independent learners. They may not have critical viewing skills and may not be able to assimilate the component parts of instructional packages into a complete learning experience (Brown 1980). Academic leaders should be prepared to assist these students with these new skills.

These students are by and large *independent* learners and require or request very little extra help. What they do want is accurate information, simplified registration procedures, easy access to faculty and support staff, and clearly defined course requirements (Julian 1982). These are needs reflective of those expressed by adult students generally.

In examining the issue for colleges of resource management much attention has been focused on making courses and faculty "cost-effective" and introducing accountability into the teaching process. Educational administrators talk about maximizing faculty productivity to serve more students with fewer "faculty resources." Technology provides alternatives to classroom lectures such as individualized packages or teleconferencing facilities allowing instructors to interact with students distant from campus (Sitton 1984). An equally important consideration, however, is maximizing student progress and making the educational process cost-effective for students. Industry training programs already totally endorse this concept (Tucker 1984). Why should the students of today have to fit into an outmoded system of "seat-time" as the measure of progress in educational institutions? Industry training and their own outside educational experiences tell them that fast track instruction offers them quicker movement into the job market saving them time and money. Funding based on credit hours encourages colleges to keep students in traditional tracks rather than offering them "self-paced" course options. This issue must be faced squarely in the very near future or all attempts to respond to the opportunity of accelerated movement that technologies allow will be sidetracked by the traditional methods of student accounting and formula funding (McCabe 1981).

Financial officers' understanding of the issues of instructional technologies will be crucial. Specific issues related to resource allocation come to the forefront quickly in discussions of instructional telecommunications and these are different from those related to more traditional instructional activity. The selection and acquisition of software and hardware may require different purchase or lease arrangements. If purchasing agents and business officers are supportive of these new financial arrangements, the college can more easily and quickly make use of the materials and technologies.

Student support services personnel are also important to the process of integrating the technologies into the mainstream of instruction. Support services to the "distance" learners or those involved in other alternative instruction may take a different form than for traditional students. However, these services must be made available for those distance learners who want and need to feel more tied to the institution. Information about support services such as career counseling, library services, etc. should be provided. This may assist and encourage distance students, many of whom enter college via telecommunications courses and later move into further programs of study on campus.

Registration procedures for these students must be convenient and flexible. Distance students may not be able to register on traditional registration day. Mail or telephone registration or continuous enrollment are options that have worked well. Off-campus or first-class registration are also options. Streamlined admissions or special student status should be available for people who are drawn to these courses by their need for the content and convenience. This requires flexibility to be designed into regular admissions and registration procedures.

Providing support services to students in technology-based courses will be provided through a director and staff. A recent national survey of community colleges indicated that the two most critical factors that contributed to or hindered telecourse use were overall institutional support and support to faculty (Dirr and others 1980). Institutions not prepared to set up and maintain an on-going service center for telecourse students are not prepared to adequately support them. Mail or telephone contact, newsletters, computer-managed correspondence and testing services, follow-up surveys, etc. are all possible pieces of the support system.

The promotion of technology-based courses should be tied to the total marketing effort of the institution. Most colleges are promoting their regular programs to reach all potential students—the "reverse transfer" student (those with four year degrees), the adult making career changes, professionals continuing their education, women entering the work force, retired and older adults and high school students. These and others formerly excluded from on-campus instruction: the handicapped, incarcerated or home-bound; and those with erratic work schedules or family responsibilities are also documented consumers of distance learning courses. Many of these potential students are drawn to telecourses related to career or technical skills, as well as to core courses for degree programs. Getting this information into the homes of those "new" students may require new strategies.

CONCLUSION

As education becomes easier to access, the shift will continue from generalized entry level content to more emphasis on job-skills, career development and vocational and technical training. People are now seeking practical skills, specialized industrial training and individual career path planning. Many will not need mass-produced education but will have available individualized and repeatable educational experiences. At the same time, however, Naisbitt's "high tech/high touch" dilemma (1984) will keep us involved in human support for these new educational experiences. Other futurists also expect that the degree of human fulfillment will be the critical criterion for assessing the quality of education. Butler (1982) says of educators, "If we are ever to be successful as educational technologists, we must learn that technology is not education . . . We must also learn that education is not instruction, but the art of being human."

Instructional technologies will require new strategies for management, faculty, and students. Preparing to manage and support these new roles and responsibilities must be a priority of the institution. Serving the needs of adult learners with new strategies, technologies and support systems will be worth the effort in the information age and beyond.

The Future

The future will bring smaller and faster computer systems, more combinations of technologies, more variety, and lower costs. The rapid rate of technological change will continue. According to Ballenger (1984) "If it's for sale today, it's obsolete."

Costs of computer systems should decline at a rate of 10-20% annually in the next several years especially in the areas of memory and data storage devices. Systems should become office size (often desktop), and will be able to operate in a normal office environment. This should eliminate the cold computer rooms which are prevalent today. Interactive, multi-functional operator workstations will enable a wide variety of activities to be performed by a single operator in a single area. Communications between workstations, campuses, states and countries via satellite and laser video techniques will be commonplace. Electronic mail and message communication within the institutional system will emerge very rapidly. On-line registration, infrequently utilized today, will be the accepted standard. Hardware will be easier to use. Keyboards have already given way to touch screens and mouse-type pointers. One prediction calls for the elimination of touch activated input devices in favor of voice activated devices by the 1990s (Chachra 1984).

The conventional languages as we know them today will be replaced by highly sophisticated programming productivity tools and languages which will automate the writing of program code as we know it. This will afford end users more flexibility in creating custom application packages. It should also allow vendors to offer better-fitting, more comprehensive software solutions to institutional needs. This will not happen without an increasing cost factor, however, as software costs should rise by the same amount as hardware costs decline. A prediction is that by the 1990s, 90% of all computer related costs within an institution will be in the areas of software and personnel (Chachra 1984).

The same change will be reflected in other technologies. Colleges will be required to sort through a variety of technologies and choose appropriate ones to best serve their needs, their students and their service area. Hardware costs will decline as computer chips and memory continue to increase in capacity and functionality. The explosion of computer, video and audio software will keep the cost of these items within a reasonable range. Satellite delivery of educational programming will vastly increase. In the short term, video recorders in the home will give students the true flexibility and convenience broadcast and cable-cast now offer to a limited degree. Personal computers will add to the delivery options with on-call video and teletex courses already available. Students will demand training relevant to their job requirements or human relation needs. Instruction will occur wherever students are: at home, at work, in community centers, in their cars, boats, planes, wherever satellite dishes, videodisk players, telephones or micro-computers are located. Education will become more interactive and more learner controlled. More attention will be paid to individual learning styles in the wide range of options available.

Funding policies will change to support more technology and will also diversify as community colleges seek new linkages with business and government. Information systems technology will force changes in policies related to all areas of the institution including faculty loads, class size, FTE funding and support services (Campbell and Ballenger 1984).

IMPLICATIONS

Adequate response to available technology will require adaptations at all levels for community colleges. In order to survive and support the commitment to excellence, leaders must be cognizant of and plan for the implications of the imminent revolutions in computers and telecommunications, which are listed below:

Administrative Computing

- To facilitate decision-making, complete, concise and timely delivery of data will be necessary. This will require attention to data systems designs and structures that allow access to information by all constituent users.
- Accessible data is helpful only if it contains the right kind of information. Long-range strategic planning will be required by administrators using needs assessments, market surveys, advisory groups and other information and

human resources to their full advantage. This planning should relate innovative opportunities of technology to the fundamental mission of the college.

- In assessing management needs, administrators must move from defining needs to developing or purchasing software, and only then to selection of appropriate hardware.
- Computer systems are only as valuable as the qualifications of the operators. Personnel training will be as critical a component of the system as the hardware and software.
- The institution will need a qualified and competent head of computing in order to successfully survive the emergence into the computer and information society. Whether this person develops from within or comes from the private sector he must be constantly aware of this role as a supportive mechanism to the instructional function. The mission of the institution must also be reflected in this position.

Instructional Technology

- More alliances between business, industry, government and educational agencies will expand the availability of information and provide alternative instructional opportunities as well. Colleges will need to adapt their informational and instructional systems to consortial arrangements. This will allow for greater numbers of instructional delivery options with input from new user groups.
- Available instructional and information technologies should be critically examined to determine the "fit" with the college mission, resources available, student, faculty and community needs. Colleges are already making mistakes by embracing the newest electronic teaching tool without carefully planning for implementation and long-term support.
- The impact of technological innovation on established instructional policies and procedures will be great. "Credit hour" value will give way to evaluation of outcomes via exit competency exams. Instructional resources will be redirected into hardware and software with faculty taking on different roles. Formula funding will be reexamined for more appropriate systems linked to the new resources needed. Credit transfer policies will expand to recognize the variety of course options available and will also be linked to competency exams.
- Instructional innovation will require new managerial, instructional and learning strategies. Administrators must set up appropriate operations to promote, support and fund instruction by telecommunication. Faculty will need incentives such as release time, access to hardware and special training opportunities to comfortably accept and adapt to the new role of coordinator and mentor. Students also must be provided assistance to use new learning strategies and new instructional systems.
- As more educational materials are produced outside the educational institution, attention must be paid to design principles which ensure instructional validity. Faculty and instructional design specialists should be given release time within the institution to develop appropriate educational experiences for their students. The cost of software development will tempt us to give away the material design and production process. Strategies must be maintained which will allow and encourage in-house materials production and bring

back the benefits to the institution.

- The varieties of instructional technologies will require more attention to research on individual learning styles. New ways of diagnosing learners' needs and prescribing instructional activities will concentrate the amazing number of options into individually designed packages which are learner controlled.

CONCLUSION

It is true, even cliched, that technology is ushering in a new age for education. Although nothing will replace the age-old individualized learning tool, the book, it will be complemented by a range of other options. The one room schoolhouse and governess/tutor have been replaced by level upon level in the public education system. Private, public and proprietary colleges, industry training programs and personal development activities provide a plethora of educational opportunities. Adults will expect colleges to provide instruction that is meaningful, convenient, timely and self-directed. Administrators and managers have a key to immeasurably expand information processing and decision making skills if they plan and implement well. Faculty and students have a key to choosing, directing and controlling their own teaching and learning activities. Technology is the key.

Reviewers for this Chapter

Thomas R. Rickman
Account Manager
Infocel
Raleigh, North Carolina

Augusta A. Julian
Executive Assistant to the President
Durham Technical Institute
Durham, North Carolina

REFERENCES

Adult Learning Service. *Promotion Packet.* Washington, D.C.: Public Broadcast Service, 1984.

Andersen, C. C. "Improving Decision Making – Computers and Information Systems." Paper presented at the Presidents' Leadership Institute, Wayne Community College, Goldsboro, North Carolina, January 1984.

Ballenger, W. L. "Future of Computers in the Future of the Community College." Paper presented at the Presidents' Leadership Institute, Wayne Community College, Goldsboro, North Carolina, January 1984.

Bender, L. W., and L. P. Conrad. "Colleges Bent on Computers Benefit from NDEA Glitches." *Community and Junior College Journal* 53, no. 8 (May 1983a): 20-23.

_____. "Fledgling, Apprentice, or Sophisticate?" *Community and Junior College Journal* 54, no. 6 (March 1984b): 30-33.

Bender, L. W. "Improving Decision Making - Computers and Information Systems." Paper presented at the Presidents' Leadership Institute, Wayne Community College, Goldsboro, North Carolina, January 1984.

Butler, D. W. "Forecasting the 80s and Beyond." *Training and Development Journal* 36, no. 12 (November 1982): 65-70.

Cameron, K. S. "Organizational Adaptation and Higher Education." *Journal of Higher Education* 55, no. 2 (March/April 1984): 122-44.

Campbell, D. F. "New Challenges for Leadership." *Community College Review* 10, no. 4 (Spring 1983): 12-17.

Campbell, D. F., and W. L. Ballenger. "The Future of Microcomputers in Community Colleges." In *Microcomputer Applications in Administration and Instruction,* New Directions for Community Colleges, no. 47. San Francisco: Jossey—Bass, 1984: 101-107.

Chachra, V. "Computing: What a Financial Officer Should Know." Paper presented at the National Council of Community College Business Officials Workshop, American Association of Community and Junior Colleges Convention, Washington, D.C., April 1983.

Conrad, L. P., and L. W. Bender. *Computers and Information Systems in the Two-Year College.* Tallahassee, Florida: Institute for Higher Education, College of Education, Florida State University, 1983.

Dirr, P., et al. *Instructional Uses of Television by Two-Year Colleges. 1978-79. Adult Learning and Broadcasting.* Washington, D.C.: American Association of Community and Junior Colleges, 1980.

Duffy, D. L., and P. F. Fendt. "Trends in Adult Learning: Implications for Community College Educators." *Community College Review* 12, no. 1 (Summer 1984): 41-47.

Jones, D. P. *Data and Information for Executive Decisions in Higher Education.* Boulder, Colorado: National Center for Higher Education Management Systems, 1982.

Julian, A. A. *Utilizing Telecommunications for Non-Traditional Instruction in the North Carolina Community College System.* Unpublished report (ED 224 957), 1982.

Lewis, R. J. *Meeting Learners' Needs Through Telecommunications.* Washington, D.C.: American Association of Higher Education, 1983.

Luskin, B. J. "Telecourses: 20 Myths 21 Realities." *Community and Junior College Journal* 53, no. 8 (May 1983): 48-60.

McCabe, R. H. "Now is the Time to Reform the American Community College." *Community and Junior College Journal* 51, no. 8 (May 1981): 6-10.

Mirkin, B. "Vo-Tech TV OK." *Community and Junior College Journal* 53, no.2 (October 1982): 36-37.

Naisbitt, J. *Megatrends: Ten New Directions Transforming Our Lives.* New York: Warner Books, 1984.

Sitton, V. "History and Evolution of the Procedures Used in the Establishment of the Individualized Instruction Center at Isothermal Community College." Paper presented at the Presidents' Leadership Institute, Coastal Carolina Community College, Jacksonville, North Carolina, May 1984.

Tucker, M. "Ruminations on Information Technology and Education." Paper presented at the Instructional Telecommunications Consortium Conference, Boston, Massachusetts, 1984.

Walker, D. "Tight Budgets and 'Socialistic' Image Plague Britain's Open University." *Chronicle of Higher Education* 28, no. 5 (1984).

Zigerell, J. J., and H. M. Chausow. *Chicago's TV College: A Fifth Report.* Chicago, Ill.: City Colleges of Chicago, 1974.

Zigerell, J. J. "A Brief Historical Survey." In *Using Mass Media for Learning,* ed. R. Yarrington. Washington, D.C.: American Association of Community and Junior Colleges, 1979: 16-18.

Chapter 6

RESOURCE DEVELOPMENT AND MARKETING

Researcher,
Barbara J. Keener
Director of Career Planning Services
The American College Testing
  Program
Aurora, Colorado

Practitioner,
John T. Blong
President
Scott Community College
Eastern Iowa Community College
  District
Bettendorf, Iowa

Principal Resource Persons Reviewed in this Chapter

RATIONALE

The role of resource development in community colleges is really the role of marketing in development as it fits into our institutional purpose. Resource development is really a form of marketing. It is a way of presenting institutions to the public for their promotion. The two are directly integrated in terms of the overall approach that institutions take with our publics and constituencies.

Barbara Kenner

Marketing and fund raising go together. Everything accomplished today should lead to the following statement: We must be proactive; we can no longer react to the environment. The same thing is true in marketing as in fund raising: people do not give to unsuccessful ventures. If you want to ruin a fund drive, tell people you're poor folk, and you're having big-time trouble, and you can't get the job done. Nobody is going to invest in that. It's so critical that everyone in the institution feels a part of marketing and deals as if they were a marketer. Nothing else is important if the staff isn't involved in marketing.

John Blong

All organizations in society, whether business or non-business in nature, offer some kind of product to some kind of consumer and, more or less, use marketing activities to further consumer acceptance . . . The choice is whether to do it (marketing) well or poorly.

L. Berry

OBJECTIVES:

By the end of this unit the reader should be able to:

- Understand the historical precedents, as well as the present context and future implications of resource development and marketing in community colleges.
- Understand the relationship between resource development and marketing and all other community college functions.
- Identify current and emerging sources of information, i.e., agencies and publications, to contact for assistance in resource development and marketing in community colleges.

INTRODUCTION

Every article written on the community college in the current decade either begins with or refers to the financial hard times that have befallen the two-year public institution in the 80's.

If present leaders can respond to present imperatives for leadership with the insight, perseverance and innovation of their predecessors, the future of the community college will be brighter than its past, which has been a shining example of American creativity and ingenuity.

Two methods of response to present challenges - resource development and marketing - were fringe endeavors of the movement through its infancy and adolescence. However, these two aspects of management response to current problems have now become imperatives.

Resource development and marketing in community colleges was one of seven areas featured in the 1983-84 Presidents' Leadership Institute, sponsored by N. C. State University for community college presidents in the state. For this segment of the seminars, Barbara J. Keener of American College Testing Program, Iowa and Vice-President of Programs for the National Council for Resource Development, and John Blong, president of Scott Community College, Iowa, were principal resource facilitators.

Blong links the functions of resource development and marketing in community colleges. To fully develop the college's resources, Blong states the entire institution must be involved in the marketing effort, and everybody in the institution must *think* marketing.

Keener says the biggest change in the last ten years of community college history is that the institutions are getting into external fund raising. She states that resource development is an exemplary manifestation of the community college movement in that it represents another new frontier to be conquered. Community colleges cannot turn to the theory and research of the past in resource development for community colleges because these fields did not exist historically.

Resource development for public two-year colleges is possibly the most crucial challenge for institutions that have met so many challenges in their short history.

Researcher

At the Presidents' Leadership Institute, Barbara J. Keener, a former development officer, focused on the practical questions, approaches and strategies regarding resource development and thereby marketing for community colleges. She answered the question, "Why get involved in resource development?" by stressing the necessity of resource development and marketing for the purposes of 1) building acceptance for the institution in the community, 2) providing quality to students, and 3) obtaining financial support for operation and growth of the institution.

Three conditions for sound development programs are essential, says Keener:
1. The college must have a blueprint that includes its history, goals and needs.
2. There must be an active core of people who believe in the program: president and development staff.
3. The college must have a carefully planned development program to include a timetable of action.

Mentioning research in the area of characteristics that contribute to success in private fund raising, Keener says that the community college possesses only one of four characteristics generally needed. The four hallmarks of successful institutions in fund raising are 1) they have wealth of their own; 2) they are large; 3) they enjoy a high socio-economic level of clientele; and 4) they offer quality programs. The community college can claim only the last characteristic; however, it has never had as a part of its missions and goals the former three.

If the community college has only one of four characteristics needed, Keener suggests coping by the use of the following strategies:
- Make sure the trustees of the college "buy into" the fund raising strategies employed by the institution.
- Establish a clear and effective institutional direction toward fund raising to include a college foundation.
- Insure that all involved understand the college foundation is the most effective way logistically to accomplish what the institution needs to do.

Because the college foundation is the most effective strategy for fund raising, Keener says the following guidelines should be used in establishing the foundation:
- Define the nature and role of the foundation: explain why it is being created, what it will do and how it relates to the organization.
- Give a clearcut explanation of relationships: what kinds of duties are necessary for the trustees, the college business officer, the president and others in the college regarding the foundation.
- Clarify college policy and direction: the institution and how it relates to the whole mission statement is a part of what is happening in the foundation.
- Establish by-laws and articles of incorporation for the foundation.
- Establish cooperative agreements for the work to be done by the foundation among all involved.
- Maintain a professional development staff and insure that all involved have professional attitudes.

Accepting the given that the foundation is essential to contemporary fund raising in community colleges, the next logical question is "Who should be selected to serve on the foundation board to insure the greatest chance of success?" Keener believes the key phrase here is that directors should give, get or get off. Less abrasively, Kenner states directors should come from the community power structure (often the informal leaders). They should have wealth themselves or be in contact with those who do; and they should be willing to give time and energy, i.e., get involved in foundation activities.

She suggests that colleges just forming foundations select a board of directors of around twenty members. Larger boards (usually already in place) must reorganize to form an active nucleus of members, but strive to keep in touch with other, less active members. Elected officials should be avoided in the selection of boards because of the uncomfortable political positions foundation fund raising activities could cause for them; and, likewise, because they may tend to be less effective in their efforts for the school.

Keener shows the direct relationship in the effectiveness of the development program to the commitment of the president of the institution to this effort, and to the extent to which it is integrated into the overall operations of the institution. She states that the president is the most important person in development and marketing efforts, followed next by the resource development officer.

Who should be a resource development officer? Keener says that the perfect resource development officer knows the institution (its missions, philosophy, goals, history and programs) and is knowledgeable of and skilled in dealing with grant writing, corporate and private foundations and marketing practices. However, such an individual is a rare find. Usually, the neophyte development officer has one qualification or the other, but not both. This situation requires that the institution give time and allocate resources for the training of new development officers so they may acquire the requisite skills to be totally effective.

In conclusion, Keener believes "the role of resource development in community colleges is really the role of marketing in development as it fits into institutional purpose. Resource development is really a form of marketing. It is a way of presenting our institutions to the public for their promotion. The two are directly integrated in terms of the overall approach that institutions take with our publics and constituencies"(Keener 1984).

Keener states that target publics, those served by the college, must understand what community colleges have to offer them: this is marketing. They must also identify and obtain what they need in terms of human, material and technological resources to be able to continue their offerings: this is resource development. Then, community colleges must persuade the target publics that they must assist with providing funding if the quality and quantity of services desired and needed are to continue: this is resource development through marketing of the institution.

Practitioner

John Blong, President of Scott Community College in Iowa, spoke from the presidential perspective at the President's Leadership Institute. Blong pointed to the necessity of changing the model used in the past relating to marketing the community college.

> I think you have to realize that we can no longer look at the inside of our institutions alone. We have to look at the environment that surrounds them. We're going to be looking at those tools which best deal with that external impact. In Iowa this year, for instance, we took a 2.8% cut in our budget during the middle of the year, and that cut will not be restored. That phenomenon is happening all over the country. We must also take a look at the socio-cultural environment: there are value changes; there are trends happening. When you look at our institutions, you have to admit there is dramatic change, and that change is impacting our institutions. Good marketing, good development are based upon the concept of dealing with the environment as well as the internal part of the institution.

Blong says the model used historically by the community college for marketing was the product orientation model. This model included the following concepts:

- Narrow definition of the nature of the business.
- Producer decides what will be produced.
- Assumption that a product will continue in demand forever.
- Emphasis on selling or "pushing" products to the consumer.
- Assumption that consumers can be induced to buy anything through sales-stimulating devices.

The model advocated by Blong for current promotion of community colleges is the marketing orientation model. He refers to Mitterich, former president of General Electric, who states, "The principal task of marketing is not so much to be skillful in making the customer do what suits the interest of the business as to be skillful in making the organization do what suits the interest of the customer."

The marketing orientation assumes the following concepts:
- Consumer needs form the basis for product development.
- Promotion is based upon consumer research.
- The assumption is that demand for a product will continue only as long as it satisfies consumer needs.
- The emphasis is on consumer "pull," not on producer "push."

Blong relates the marketing orientation concepts to educational marketing of programs. In this model, he says, external forces (students, society) dominate the emphasis. Strategic planning is essential, and this strategy must include attempts to satisfy existing markets as well as create new markets. The operative term in the marketing model is flexibility. As in the past, the community college can expect to be required to adapt to changes in the environment with a readiness not expected of any other institution of higher learning. The present imperative for a shift to marketing orientation is a shift from the reactive (defensive) marketing techniques of the past to a proactive (offensive) stance in competing for students.

Blong says that leaders must re-think the way they look at their institutions. The top people in academics, finance and administrative positions must take a new approach to promoting the institution and should include the person in charge of marketing and resource development in the decision making processes. He even suggests that the chief executive of the community college be the chief marketer. Marketing requires the strong public relations skills essential to have gotten the CEO where he or she is. So logically, the CEO is best equipped to handle the marketing responsibilities. If this is not possible, at least the marketing person should be placed in the next highest level of administration.

Blong's approach to resource development and marketing, then, essentially is two-pronged: 1) have at the focus of all marketing strategies, the needs of the target markets and 2) place the responsibility for resource development and marketing as close to the top of the decision making hierarchy as possible.

Blong refers to the marketing concept as including goal directed behavior, consumer needs orientation, integrated effort and socially responsible behavior. In alluding to the commonly held belief that marketing educational institutions is somehow unethical, he points to the fact that education has been marketing its product since the beginning through catalogs, brochures, even word of mouth. The difference and the ethical component of what Blong advocates is that the emphasis and effort of an ethical approach to marketing is that the student (target population) and his needs must be at the forefront of all marketing decisions and approaches. Previous to this, if the student is at the forefront of all programming decisions, there cannot then be anything unethical in promoting these programs in the most effective way.

Blong believes in using the classic marketing strategies of differentiation, segmentation and positioning for marketing educational programs. He uses the analogy of employing a rifle, not a shotgun, in marketing approaches. Community colleges must differentiate the population into the group which can be served by the particular institution in question. Then, the several segments which will require different services from the institution must be identified. And finally, the institution must position itself to be able to provide the services required by its markets. This, Blong says is responsive and responsible marketing.

Although Blong sees the integral relationship between marketing and resource development, he deferred the indepth discussion of resource development to Keener because of her experience as a practitioner in the field. He did, however, state that marketing and fund raising go together. He also pointed to the direct relationship of the success of resource development efforts to the success of the marketing efforts of the college. No one, he says, is going to invest in an unsuccessful venture. Marketing stresses the strengths of the institution and resource development stresses the ways in which the strong aspects of the institution can become even stronger. One is intrinsically related to the other.

IMPLICATIONS

". . . all questions of curriculum, students and institutional mission (in the community colleges) pale in light of funding issues" (Cohen and Brawer 1982). Cohen and Brawer point out that when community colleges were small and required only a public pittance for full operation, no one questioned or cared to know how they were financed. But because community colleges enroll fully half of all people who enter college for the first time, a very close scrutiny of funding patterns for these institutions is now in order.

The 1980s have brought new challenges. The community college has been tapped to serve as the primary in-place resource to provide training necessary to move the industrial society into the information age. Concurrently, while performing this transformation, the community college will be required to produce more efficiently with reduced funding and will be held strictly accountable: ergo, the necessity for resource development.

Dale Parnell, President of the American Association of Community and Junior Colleges (AACJC) believes that community colleges are between the high school and the university and, therefore, "are uniquely situated at the crossroads in the community to provide much of the linkage leadership" essential today. He feels that the tremendous challenge facing the community college today is that of clarifying the image of these institutions. He uses the analogy of a fuzzy image on a slide show: too many citizens across the nation, he feels, have a fuzzy image of the community. He wants to "turn the knob" and clarify the image (Parnell 1984).

Parnell also talks of competition in the educational market place and says the community colleges must know how to market their product. This is a competence that leadership must master. Methods for responding to the ever-increasing competition for scarce resources are emerging in regard to community colleges. Turk (1984) suggests that in order to be successful in any competitive environment, the institution must stress its uniqueness. Experts in marketing, he says, explain uniqueness as carving a niche which separates the particular institution from all others providing similar services. Turk states that the stage is set for combining the concepts of strategic planning and traditional marketing: strategic marketing.

Strategic marketing involves:
- Analysis of the environment.
- Needs assessment.
- Analysis of the competition.
- Determination of strengths and weaknesses.
- Preparation of a clear statement of mission, goals, objectives and strategies.
- Development of programs and services to satisfy needs.
- Determination of pricing and delivery to target markets.

Strategic marketing offers a new approach to the new problems of marketing institutions that are facing institutions today.

Roueche and Baker (1983) state that "college personnel and governing boards must understand and support the concept of marketing, or marketing campaigns will be doomed from the outset." They cite Johnson who points out that marketing techniques used historically by educational institutions have dealt characteristically with serving the institution and not its clientele. Echoing Blong, Roueche and Baker believe "the marketing-oriented college will meet individual needs, ensuring the success of learners in both academic and personal endeavors."

Chaffee (1984) refers to the adaptive model of strategic management which "involves attuning the organization to changes in market demands and reorienting the organization as needed in order to maintain or increase the flow of resources from the market to the organization. On the basis of this model, colleges . . . have been advised to conduct market research, monitor trends in their environment, increase their flexibility . . . ., and update their program offerings." She also alludes to Kotler and Murphy who have offered what she says may be the most adaptive model yet presented. Kotler and Murphy state "with the growing shortage of students, the challenge facing the president is to develop a marketing orientation with the faculty in which everyone sees his or her job as sensing, serving, and satisfying markets."

Strategic planning implies not only the "what" aspects of the future, but also the "how." This is the entrance point for resource development. "Only those institutions with the ability to adjust to the challenge of the future will survive into the twenty-first century" (Dunn 1983).

The North Carolina Council of Officers for Resource Development (CORD) published a 1983 membership report showing a little over half of the schools in the 58-school system have established a resource development position. The listing did not indicate whether development was the only administrative responsibility of these people. However, the existence of this organization and its counterparts in other states shows the growing understanding of the importance of resource development to fulfilling the promises of the community college.

On the national level, the National Council for Resource Development (NCRD), an affiliate of the American Association of Community and Junior Colleges (AACJC), provides assistance and continuity for resource development programs. Founded in 1972, NCRD states its purpose as facilitating and promoting the efforts of two-year college funding activities. With over 600 members, ten regional organizations and many state affiliates, NCRD focuses on providing services and increasing equity in federal funding patterns.

The new stress on resource development and marketing for the community college is a result of the institution's evolving mission. Nespoli and Martorana (1983-84) see two trends that impact on financing the evolving missions of the community college: 1) not whether life-long learning and community activities are a part of the mission, but who should finance them, and 2) re-emphasis on state financing of local institutions. They continue to say that individuals responsible for allocations are not convinced of the worth of community education and therein lies the potential for crisis.

Currently, community college leaders are looking for viable ways to make good the promise stated in the mission of these institutions. Resource development and marketing are increasingly being perceived as vehicles for response to fiscal restraints, accountability imperatives and the call for creative and innovative approaches to problem solving. However, the need for top-down affirmation of the importance of these programs must be recognized if they are to be effective and efficient.

The role of the community college president in resource development and marketing is generally accepted as being at the forefront of all efforts (Blong 1984). In the *Chronicle of Higher Education,* David Daniel, president of Wilkes Community College in North Carolina, states "resource development should be central to all your operations, never an appendage." He sees involvement with the community as a primary presidential imperative. "No one can take the place of the president in fund raising. I spend half my time away from the college doing just that."

In the same article, Robert L. Stoddard, dean of development and former acting president at Snow College, Utah, says the Snow College "president spends one-third of his time working on development."

The next most important person in the development program is the person in charge of resource development. David Hodge (1981), assistant vice-president for development at Baptist College in Charleston, S.C., says the two main roles of the development person are first, to act as the college's liaison with any and all gift or grant awarding individuals or agencies and second, to assist college personnel in acquiring necessary resources.

Hodge lists twenty-two characteristics essential for successful development officers. Although the development officer is in a pivotal position concerning successful program efforts, the most critical task to be performed by this person is communicating the comprehensive development program to the other college personnel, states Keener. She says that certainly one development officer, and even a development officer and modest staff, cannot possibly conduct a successful development program without full approval and support from all college staff members.

IMPLICATIONS

Commitment that begins with the president of the institution, responsibility for the overall program resting with the resource development officer, and a knowledgeable and supportive faculty and staff are all essential ingredients for a resource development plan which is brought to fruition through effective marketing strategies.

This is the present contextual understanding of experts in the field relating to how community colleges can respond to future expectations of increased demands and decreased funding. For those institutions who do not presently have resource development and marketing programs in place, the time to begin is now. Those institutions with these programs already in place need to fine tune these vehicles of support for the hard times ahead.

Resource development in a comprehensive approach encompasses pursuing federal, state and private foundation grants; establishing a college foundation for the pursuit of unencumbered funds; conducting an annual fund drive to include planned gifts, corporate gifts, major gifts, special gifts, mini campaigns, an on-campus drive and special events; telling the story of institutional needs and services through development publications; providing financial assistance to students through scholarships and loan funds; recruiting students to enhance governmental funding allocations; and other related activities.

CONCLUSION

Marketing the institution encompasses all the action strategies employed to plan, implement and evaluate the comprehensive resource development program of the institution. Resource development through marketing is essential if the opportunity to provide excellence in the future of community colleges is to be grasped by present community college leadership personnel.

Marketing

Any sound marketing textbook will give the basics of marketing which are essentially the same for toothpaste, automobiles and education. Marketing literature that deals only with community colleges is scarce. Because this emerging field is so new, the most helpful writings to date tend to be dissertations which offer good backgrounds in marketing theory and applied research, papers presented at education conferences and descriptive reports. Following are examples of these: (ERIC numbers are given in parentheses)

Smith, J. D., et al. *A Survey and Market Research Activities in Two- and Four-Year Colleges and Universities.* Cleveland, Ohio: Cuyahoga Community College, 1981. (ERIC Resource Document Reproduction Service No. ED 211 164).

Dann, D. D. *The Status, Scope, and Structure of Marketing in a Selected Group of Community Colleges.* (ERIC Resource Document Reproduction Service No. ED 231 443).

Parsons, M. H. *Where Do We Go From Here? The Use of the Market Analysis Survey in Needs Assessment and Program Development.* Paper presented at the National Conference on "Needs Assessment: The Pulse of the Community," Blacksburg, Virginia, May 11, 1982. (ERIC Resource Document Reproduction Service No. ED 217 909).

Carling, C., G. J. Ryan, and G. Jeremiah (eds.) *Report of the 1982 Marketing Committee.* Lindcroft, N. J.: Brookdale Community College, October 14, 1982 (ERIC Resource Document Reproduction Service No. 224 516).

Wilhelmi, C., et al. *Marketing Plan 1983-84.* Annandale, Virginia: Northern Virginia Community College, June 30, 1983. (ERIC Resource Document Reproduction Service No. ED 234 839).

Books dealing with marketing community colleges are not plentiful. However, the two following are very helpful.

Heim, W. A. and C. Keim. *Marketing the Program.* New Directions for Community Colleges, San Francisco: Jossey-Bass, (eds.) 1981.

Harrold, R. *Economic Thinking in Education.* University of New England Press, 1982. Gives an economist's perspective in thinking through choices in use of time, planning and resource utilization.

Because of the close connection between resource development and marketing, it can be expected that NCRD will be responding increasingly to the interest in marketing community colleges with seminars and reprints.

In March 1984, the Center for Responsive Governance in Washington, D.C. hosted a three-day conference, "Marketing for Non-Profit Organizations." The conference included sessions dealing with an overview of marketing, strategic planning, target market identification, legal issues and others.

The National Planned Giving Institute offered a one-week seminar on "Designing and Implementing a Successful Planned Giving Program and Marketing the Planned Giving Program" at several different times and locations during the first six months of 1984. Although dealing with only one aspect of a comprehensive development program, this type of seminar indicates the dawning recognition of marketing's importance to development.

Marketing has an organic relationship with resource development. As interest in each field, as it relates to community colleges, continues to grow, complementary growth will occur in the other.

Resource Development

Appendix D lists agencies and publications (with addresses) dealing with resource development. Knowledge of these is considered essential for the resource development officer.

The volume of publications relating to resource development in general, and specifically relating to community colleges, is overwhelming. Numerous books have been written on every aspect of resource development, and papers and descriptive reports abound. No attempt will be made here to cover the field, but several agencies and publications will be highlighted. No attempt is made to prioritize the listing by value of agencies or publications or to be inclusive.

The Foundation Center in New York City has offered assistance in philanthropic giving to non-profit organizations for twenty-eight years. Providing regional branch services, this agency offers publications, seminars and workshops on foundations and their giving practices, and is an organization founded by these organizations, so it is obviously an authoritative source. Of principal interest are *The Foundation Directory* and *Foundation Grants Index*.

The Council for Advancement and Support of Education (CASE) is a national organization serving as a principal public affairs arm for education, logically, therefore, supporting the endeavors of resource development. CASE holds national conferences, publishes newsletters and holds workshops on timely topics. It also makes yearly awards for outstanding performances by member institutions.

The Fund-Raising Institute (FRI) offers assistance on all aspects of fund-raising. Publications and seminars touch on techniques for successful fund raising ranging from working with institutional foundations to conducting phone-a-thons. Of particular value is the *FRI Annual Giving Book* by M. Jane Williams, which gives complete information on conducting sustained annual giving campaigns.

"The Grantsmanship Center is a non-profit educational institution that provides more training and publications on the art of grantsmanship, direct fund raising, management and development of resources than any other organization in the country," quoting from a letter from Norton J. Kiritz, president. It offers five-day training programs and a bi-monthly magazine, The Grantsmanship Center *News*, which has the largest paid circulation of non-profit publications.

Many other organizations offer similar services and are reputable sources of assistance. The Taft Corporation provides thorough information on private foundations as does the Public Management Institute, which also deals with other aspects of fund raising. *Standard and Poor's Register of Corporations, Directors and Executives* provides a source of valuable information for corporate giving campaigns.

Publications that are helpful are *The Community College Foundation,* Harvey W. Sharron, Jr., NCRD (See Appendix D); *Designs for Fund-Raising,* Harold J. Seymour; McGraw-Hill Book Company and *Gonser, Gerber, Tinker, Stuhr on Development,* by Gonser, Gerber, Tinker, Stuhr Publishers.

Interstate Securities publishes a yearly listing of the 100 largest firms headquartered in the Carolinas called *Carolinas' Companies.* Other states may offer the same service, which is helpful in identifying and locating potential corporate giving prospects.

Emerging literature includes a projected publication for the fall-winter of 1984-85 by David Daniel, president of Wilkes Community College in N.C., and Louis Bender, director of the Institute for Higher Education at Florida State University. Assisting in the effort will be Bill Davis, director of development at Wilkes. The book will be organized in three sections: 1) a conceptual background of resource development, i.e., the raison d'etre, 2) a historical perspective from a utilization of human qualities standpoint, i.e., the do's and don't's of working with people, and 3) a technical "how to" discussion, i.e., a discussion of the materials, techniques and methods of successful resource development programs.

Daniel states it is hoped that N.C.'s Council of Officers for Resource Development (CORD) will adopt the new book as a text for the annual one-week CORD internship for new development officers. The book will be updated across the years to insure its continued utility.

Daniel also says the focus of the book is on resource development as a sharing process. Whatever can be done to sharpen practices in small public institutions is worthwhile; no one is more deserving of advocacy than community colleges, he says.

Resource development is increasingly the topic of journal articles in the community college field. Of particular benefit are the *Community College Review, Community and Junior College Journal,* and the *Journal of Higher Education.* Historically these publications have offered the most recent thinking of practitioners in the field and can be expected to continue doing so.

The quality of assistance for community colleges is excellent and the quantity of materials and agencies offering assistance is growing. Staying abreast of current thinking and innovative approaches is essential for development officers as is making contacts with the authorities in the field.

Reviewer for this Chapter

Sylvia T. Pierce
Director of Curricular Research and
    Development
Fayetteville Technical Institute
Fayetteville, North Carolina

REFERENCES

Alfred, R. L. "Paradox for Community Colleges: Education in the '80's." *Community College Review* 12, no. 1 (Summer 1984): 2-6.

Berry, L. "Marketing Continuing Education Programs." *Business Education Forum* 27, no. 8 (1973).

Blong, J. "Resource Development and Marketing." Paper presented at the Presidents' Leadership Institute, Rowan Technical College, Salisbury, North Carolina, April 1984.

Chaffee, E. E. "Successful Strategic Management in Small Private Colleges." *Journal of Higher Education* 55, no. 2 (March/April 1984): 212-41.

Cohen, A. M., and F. B. Brawer. *The American Community College.* San Francisco: Jossey-Bass, 1982.

Dunn, S. L. "The Changing University: Survival in the Information Society." *The Futurist* 17, no. 4, (August 1983): 55-60.

Hodge, R. D. *The Resource Development Officer.* Washington, D.C.: National Council of Resource Development, n.d.

Jenkins, J. "More Dollars from Private Sector—Future Funding Trend." *Community and Junior College Journal* 54, no. 5 (February 1984): 24-25.

Keener, B. J. "Resource Development and Marketing." Paper presented at the Presidents' Leadership Institute, Rowan Technical College, Salisbury, North Carolina, April 1984.

Keller, G. *Academic Strategy - The Management Revolution in American Higher Education.* Baltimore: Johns Hopkins University Press, 1983.

Nespoli, L. A., and S. V. Martorana. "Tensions in Defining Community College Missions: Problem or Opportunity?" *Community College Review* 11, no. 4 (Spring 1984): 3-11.

Parnell, D. "Opportunity with Excellence: Vision of the Future." Interview by Dale F. Campbell and Robert M. Stivender, 13 June 1984. Tape recording, American Association of Community and Junior Colleges, Washington, D.C.

Roueche, J. E. and G. A. Baker III. *Beacons for Change: An Innovative Outcome Model for Community Colleges.* Iowa City, Iowa: American College Testing Program, 1983.

Sharron, H. W. Jr. (ed.) *The Community College Foundation*. Washington, D.C.: National Council For Resource Development, 1982.

Turk, F. "New Initiatives for Management: Increasing Revenues and Resources." *Business Officer* 17, no. 11 (May 1984): 17-32.

"Two-Year Colleges Step Up Their Pursuit of Private Funds." *Chronicle of Higher Education*, April 16, 1984.

Young, J. H. "Resource Development in the Community College: A Time to Rethink Priorities." *Community College Review* 8, no. 1 (Summer 1980): 24-26.

Chapter 7

INSTITUTIONAL IMPACT AND IMAGE

Researcher,
Richard L. Alfred
Associate Professor and Director of
    Community College Program
University of Michigan
Ann Arbor, Michigan

Principal Resource Person Reviewed in this Chapter

RATIONALE

Needed are new approaches to finance keyed to the use of institutional research data to describe unique impacts of community college education on students, public and private-sector organizations, the community and the state—data that can be used to rebuild the resource base of the college in periods of fiscal austerity.

Richard L. Alfred

Competition for shrinking dollars has made it imperative for all public institutions to be able to prove their value to taxpayers; analysis of the socioeconomic impact of a college on its community is one strategy for demonstration of such value.

James F. Gollattscheck

Since the early 1960's the growth and importance of impact studies to measure the economic, social and technological outcomes produced by post-secondary institutions has accelerated as tensions rise among competitive providers for future support by funding agenices and legislative decision-makers. Richard Alfred of the University of Michigan, in speaking to the Presidents' Leadership Institute, explained the crisis in community college education as one of moderating revenues into the 1990's, as such institutional impact assessment will play a critical role in securing state and local resources. Alfred explains the cyclical nature of impact. He maintains, "How institutions allocate money shapes the impact of the outcomes that they produce; in turn, their ability to document the nature and extent of the outcome produced has an impact on the funding obtained from external agencies."

The role impact assessment can play in buffeting predicted economic budgetary recessions should be to ease or brake the downward spiral of budgets for education by establishing documentation of performance for the community college which can be provided to both local and state revenue sources to substantiate annual budget requests. Stabilizing enrollments and dwindling resources have signaled the close of a period of growth that characterized community college development in the 1960s. Now cost effectiveness - using resources to maximize the social and economic benefits to the individual in return for investment in education - is the watchword (Alfred 1980). These requests, supported by information about the economic and social benefits offered to students and the community can, in turn, demonstrate to funding sources that in competition with universities, proprietary schools and not-for-profit corporations for students and resources, community colleges can perform favorably.

Conceptually, impact can be divided into four major areas: (1) impacts on individual students; (2) impacts on the national economy; (3) impacts on local and regional economics; and (4) general societal impacts. Probably the best documented of the four impacts is on student outcomes. Higher education has profound effects on students in economic, cognitive and attitudinal terms (Melchiori and Nash 1983). Impact assessment and the marketing of student outcomes information can become the means by which the community college can secure a position in the community as a provider of quality, cost-effective educational services. Although an optimistic scenario for community colleges involves growing demand for their services, continued political support, an ability to control costs while remaining competitive with other sectors, and a favorable fiscal climate, this scenario is unlikely in the absence of outcome data. Specific factors of importance are . . . increased political support at all levels of government, based on documented service to a broad range of constituencies, flexibility and contribution to local economic development (Breneman and Nelson 1981).

Strategic decisions in a community college using the tools of impact assessment must be made in the context of current and future state and regional conditions that affect the community. Community college administrators, faced with impact research as an adaptive strategy, must then investigate both the internal and external outcomes that make up institutional service and assess their impact. Myran (1983) explains the role choice can and will have in these and other decisions made by community college administrators in the future. He states, "More than in the past, community college leaders will create the future of their institutions by the choices that they make. And, choose they must. As the pace of technological, economic, political and social change continues to accelerate, community college leaders must choose among the external and internal stimuli that demand attention and analysis. They must choose between alternative scenarios for the development of the college in response to these stimuli, and they must choose how the limited human, physical and financial resources of the college should be developed and allocated." Making a case for uniqueness depends upon whether a particular college is facing an optimistic or pessimistic scenario regarding internal and external factors impacting the campus. How to assess and document these factors will be the focus of this chapter.

OBJECTIVES

At the end of this chapter, you should be able to:
1. Identify 5 major assumptions about your community college system which distinguish it from systems in other states. Alternately, identify several assumptions about your system which parallel systems in other states;
2. Describe the critical internal and external factors which can facilitate or constrain growth and future success in your college. Assess the direction of public policy in drawing your conclusions;
3. Based on Alfred's corrective solutions, record corrective solutions for your college, making a case for its uniqueness as a provider of educational opportunities among competitive forces.

INTRODUCTION

In his presentation to the Presidents' Leadership Institute on "Impact Assessment: Making a Case for Community Colleges," Richard Alfred presented an assessment of community colleges based on his experience as an administrator/practitioner, researcher and analyst of state and national public policy. In making a case for the community college, Alfred defined impact assessment as a reciprocal concept. On the one hand impacts are created by what colleges do with learners; how they contribute to the regional employment market; and the educational opportunities they create which convert the unemployed or unemployable into taxpaying citizens yielding revenues to the state and locality. On the other side of this framework for impact assessment is the impact made upon the college by conditions in the external environment such as reduced resources, increasing competition for resources and programs, increasing state control, changing federal policies, demographic transition, technological change and politicization of the institution. State funding formulas, for example, may not be tied to inflation indexes and may jeopardize the colleges' abilities to keep up with rising costs. Moreover, there has been a "loss of romance" between the local and state funding sources and the maturing community college system. Aging facilities and equipment no longer have the political appeal that gleaming and growing campuses had in the first twenty years of the community college movement.

The long-standing romance has, therefore, been squandered and replaced by the need for community colleges to address accountability issues with their funding sources and community constituencies. Accountability to funding sources, taxpayers and students marks an important transition in the direction of the colleges, moving them from a process-orientation of unlimited growth and educational opportunities to an outcome orientation of cost efficient program delivery which maximizes resources and constructively channels the debate over community college benefits and costs.

Assumptions About the Community College

In making a case for impact assessment with specific reference to the North Carolina community college system, Alfred articulated ten major assumptions about the community college system noting unique differences between this system and other state systems. Noted were conditions such as the "geographic dispersion of institutions" across the state. Within 30 miles, there are fifty-eight community colleges serving 100 counties. Secondly, North Carolina has moved from an agricultural-based economy to a manufacturing economy and is now engaged in a transition to a technological economy. In comparison with many other states, Alfred said, "North Carolina is viewed from the outside as one of the three or four national models for economic development and diversification."

Additionally, the North Carolina community colleges have no desire to limit or constrain the "open door" philosophy. Moreover, he said, "If anything, you may choose to expand access to particular population groups that are not currently served. Michigan and other northern industrial states are having to reassess the open door admissions concept because they simply cannot afford to serve every purpose for every person." Demographic restructuring too, is a major concern for these colleges. Population decline, as a whole, is not a concern in North Carolina. Serving older people - an as yet unserved and growing learner population - may possibly become one of the next major service populations, compared to 18 to 35 year-olds who comprise the majority of learners among the institutions. And this must be done to provide programs for older, working adults in a manner that does not disrupt their income (Dunn 1983).

The fifth assumption was a focus on quality education. Although it was addressed to the presidents of North Carolina community colleges, the points made by Alfred would apply to all community colleges. There is a discernible focus on quality, but faculty and administrators are not sure how to measure and define it. Palmer (1983), in his review of the literature on how quality is measured, listed five determinants of quality for the community college to consider: (1) institutional resources; (2) instructional and management processes; (3) student outcomes; (4) value-added impact on students; and (5) curricular structure and emphasis. The sixth assumption tends to support Palmer's premise about quality. Alfred indicates that a strong focus on upgrading faculty, facilities and instructional programs is a current major concern for many community colleges. Parnell (1982), holding a similar set of beliefs, advanced the issue of quality to the forefront of academia when he asked, "Is there a search for excellence on your campus? What has your academic senate done about improving teaching? What has your college done about nourishing a caring, teaching, learning environment?"

The seventh assumption dealt with unmet learner needs and student populations. Specifically, Alfred said, "There is a huge pent-up demand for adult education and adult basic education in North Carolina and I put the emphasis on the word "pent-up demand," or unmet demand. This probably will become your next population base in community colleges." Colleges and universities, nationwide, are also placing new emphasis on programs for adult basic education. Although community colleges do not have exclusive access to this large population, the advantages of pricing and easy access to service populations provides a marketable edge among competing forces.

Assumptions eight and nine deal with improved services to business and industry and improved funding for continuing education. First, closer linkages with business and industry need to be established and the private sector, as a whole, needs to have more involvement with community colleges. One means to improving linkages is the growing interest in developing consortiums: agreements between post-secondary institutions, private business and industry, public schools, human service agencies and other major community organizations. One such effort to improve needed linkages over a region covering the states of Virginia, North Carolina, and Georgia was an invitational conference, "Developing Human Capital: A Shared Responsibility," held at North Carolina State University and sponsored by the American Council on Education Commission on Higher Education and the Adult Learner. At the invitation of the Commission, educators, business and industry, and government agencies were invited to generate information and stimulate activities to assist campus leaders, public policy makers and business and industry to clarify and shape post-secondary education's role in educating adults. One major outcome, addressed by representatives of these three groups, was the need for consortia to improve linkages and to facilitate communication channels. Assumption nine raised the question of equity in funding for continuing education. Funding in North Carolina is 50 percent of an equivalent FTE which led Alfred to pose the question, "Is it worth offering continuing education in terms of financial feasibility for the college?"

Assumption ten focused on community renewal and the difference between North Carolina and other states engaged in community development activities. Noting that North Carolina had enormous promise, Alfred observed, "I find it interesting that you have the financial ability to focus on renewal of community, while other states simply don't have the financial wherewithal to accomplish this task. The question for consideration is, what specific steps are your colleges taking to provide innovative services to the community that are not, or cannot be provided by other organizations?"

Distinguishing Characteristics of the North Carolina Community College System

Despite many of the advantageous conditions present in this state for educational and community services, there are some distinguishing characteristics about the community college system that condition the environment for impact assessment. Alfred listed four major distinctions between North Carolina and other states and posed some questions about future directions:

1. The North Carolina Community College System is marked by abundant resources compared to other states;
2. The ability to keep the "open door" open still remains;
3. There are a limited number of revenue sources (i.e., the legislature) and limited opportunities for expanding the number of funding sources. Because diversification of revenue is very critical to community college education, efforts should be made to diversify revenue sources beyond the current number; and
4. There exists a "pent-up" demand of an aging learner population, many of whom have adult basic education needs. This is a key distinction. How do community colleges match a changing learner population with basic skill education not in place with a state obviously moving toward a high level of technological sophistication? There is a potential mismatch between a state moving toward technology and a huge wave of adult education learners who

have demands unmet in terms of basic education. Is it possible that social unrest could unfold in that population by the year 1990 or 1995?

External Factors in the Environment

The external environment is as important as the internal organization as a planning dimension for community colleges. The collegial structure and loosely developed performance objectives of community colleges hamper their ability to collect impact information and, in particular, to generate outcomes data on students. Apprehension too, on the part of faculty and administrators concerning the uses of college data, significantly detours them from making attempts to assess impact. Ewell (1983) in an NCHEMS study on student outcomes, describes three main reasons for this reluctance. First, there is a fear that outcomes information, if collected and widely disseminated, will reflect badly on those collecting it. Second, there is a conviction that many if not most of the important outcomes of higher education are qualitative and cannot therefore be objectively measured. And third, there is considerable apprehension about the "false precision" inherent in quantified outcomes criteria.

Adding to this fear and confusion, broader external factors exist in the community college environment, nationwide, which severely erode the ability of the institution to assess outcomes. The first factor involves the way community colleges are organized nationally; they are thought of as "classic service organizations." Their success is defined, almost universally, in terms of quantitative factors such as the size of the budget and the size of enrollment. The bigger the budget and the larger the increments per year, the more the institution is thought of as being successful. Moreover, the size of the budget is construed as evidence of success because the college becomes organized primarily in quantitative dimensions in response to its environment. Qualitative factors, alternately, are overlooked. Time and energy are not devoted to things that appear on the surface as not measurable in quantitative terms.

The internal organization of the college is not conducive to meaningful assessment of quantitative and qualitative outcomes. Nationwide, the associate degree has no uniform definition. State to state, the criteria for completion of a degree is so varied that business and industry cannot be guaranteed consistent performance by community college products. Synthesis of findings indicate that the associate degree would be more highly valued with certain modifications in the way it is defined and conferred. The first recommendation is directed toward strengthening the quality of the associate degree in order to improve its relevance and value to the student, the employers and the four-year institution to which the degree holder may wish to transfer (Koltai 1983). The lack of analytical skills training intrinsic to the liberal arts also constitutes a growing dilemma for the community college graduate. While technical skills help to get an individual the employment desired, the rapid erosion or obsolescence of technical skills may require retraining two to three years following graduation. The result is that opportunities for promotion become minimal when liberal arts skills are not present to close the gap in career development. The question that remains is who will do the retraining, the community college or the university?

And the last major environmental factor and, in most cases, the deciding factor is the eventuality of reductions in state funding in the years ahead. Coupled with increasing competition for students, this dual dimension of reduced funding and competing providers can, and will, force the community college to cope with constraints that have not been major concerns during the last two decades.

Major Questions About This Community College External Environment

Alfred posed eleven major questions that outline concerns for community colleges nationwide and in North Carolina. These questions, listed below, provide the foundation for inquiry into the current and future status of the community college as a provider of educational opportunities for their respective communities and states. Alfred's major concerns are as follows:

1. What is the cost efficiency of a community college system serving a large geographic area with a relatively small population or a small geographic area with a large population?
2. Is it possible that a relatively low cost efficiency will put all or some of the colleges in a system at a disadvantage in the quest for scarce resources with competitors such as four-year colleges, K-12 school districts, and others?
3. Are community colleges organized on the basis of dependence on year-to-year increments in budgets? Must our institutions have a 10 percent per year increase to operate or can they, in fact, absorb reductions or revenues that don't keep pace with inflation? Are community colleges organized to make reductions if necessary?
4. What strategies should be employed to develop a cohesive identity for community colleges as a provider of post-secondary educational resources? Do individual institutions go their own way when it comes down to that identity or will they coalesce as part of a "system strategy?"
5. Is the current image of the community college with external funding sources adequate to stave off challenges from human service organizations, if state revenues become scarce?
6. What are the prevailing perceptions of individual colleges held by funding sources and policy makers? Are they favorable or unfavorable and in what ways would they become more or less favorable with respect to current public policy issues for community college education?
7. Do colleges rely too heavily on a political strategy in their states to gain resources or do they have other means such as using data as a vehicle to gain resources?
8. Is there a false security in terms of current enrollment conditions and trends? Have community colleges predicated institutional planning and budgets on constantly increasing enrollment? What will happen to the budget and institutional programs if enrollment decreases?
9. Will a squeeze exist for the community college between the univeristy and K-12 school districts over the next five years in terms of funding?
10. If K-12 school districts improve the level of their remedial education and improve basic skill education, what will be the impact on the community college?
11. What will happen if four-year colleges and universities improve their delivery systems to adult learners and do so with cost efficiency and clarity so that the adult learner will prefer to enroll there because they would prefer to have the baccalaureate degree anyway?

Internal Constraints on Measuring Impact

Nationally, community colleges over the past twenty years have, by virtue of their growth and maturity, created several major constraints that *could* continue to limit the abilities of the college to gain prominence in academic and organizational renewal. These constraints constitute fundamental barriers which make faculty acceptance and participation in planning and assessment difficult, organizational decision-making in a complex environment unresponsive to change, and relationships with political constituencies less fluid than they were in an earlier decade.

In its most elemental form, the nature of the community college organization has become too process oriented. "There is too much emphasis on process and too little emphasis on outcomes," states Alfred. FTE's are what count, not the starting salary of the graduates. It's the size of the budget that really tells how successful you are, not the benefits to taxpayers of student education in a micro-electronics lab during one quarter. The need to demonstrate accountability to legislators and the public is here and, yet, numerous examples of "process" indicators remain intact as barometers of administrative priorities.

Another constraint facing community colleges is a virtual resistance to change. "We have a resistance to change that is very much a principle of an aging faculty and administrative organization," explains Alfred. "We do not have the young faculty of the formative years. Our facilities are aging and so is our equipment. Aging faculty accustomed to "guaranteed enrollments" can cause problems by their inertia." "How to deal with this problem," adds Alfred, "is to ask yourself as an adminsitrator, 'Do we have an on-going, organized staff development program to begin to get our faculty to move in new directions?' "

The "loss of romance" is still, yet another constraint between the college and its constituencies, in particular its funding sources. Alfred describes the following scenario as an inevitable reality whose time has come. "The community college is not the romantic enterprise in the eyes of legislators that it was 10 to 15 years ago . . . New buildings, new programs, new staff—building a new institution—is an enormously attractive political proposition. But, advancing budget proposals to the legislature to repair cracking mortar and leaky roofs in existing facilities, to enhance faculty salaries in programs that have been in place for 10 to 15 years, and to replace obsolete equipment is not an attractive political proposition. As a consequence of this *loss of romance*, community colleges must begin to find other politically attractive ways to appeal to legislatures and county governments as well as taxpayers in order that financial support may remain on par with the revenue growth of the past two decades. Wattenbarger (1978), using Young's (1977) set of resource development elements, suggests that in order to develop new resources, institutional decision-making and support of the college should establish priorities among available programs and provide administrative support and resource allocation to those at the top level in order to assure greater probability of outside funding.

Influencing decision-making behavior in external funding agencies also has an internal counterpart within community colleges: how to influence decision-making processes of both the administration and faculty? These groups are not as apt to change or be influenced by changing external conditions, despite the need to address changing demographics, increased competition from alternate providers, centralization of decision-making in state agencies, and greater accountability to revenue sources. Alfred defines this problem as "rigidification of the decision process." Organizational complexity has elongated and extended to a range of new constituencies decision-making processes in the community college. It takes a long time to achieve concensus on a decision made when one has to consult multiple constituencies, states Alfred. Because of the increasing levels of complexity, he adds, a president has to consult with administrators, classified staff, the faculty union, the academic senate, the curriculum committee and other groups bearing vested interest. If faced with the question, "Could the community college nationwide turn on a dime in developing a new program as in previous years?" Alfred added, "I would have to say 'no,' they cannot. There are just too many constituencies to consult because our institutions are much more complex than they used to be."

An important dimension of the decision-making process that adds an additional barrier or constraint for community college development is that of full-time faculty as partners in the academic enterprise. Faculty teach, they provide basic academic advisement and committee work and then they leave campus. Faculty are not involved in academic planning; they are not heavily involved in academic budgeting at the department level; and they are not involved in research and assessment of future manpower needs, explains Alfred. And this has serious consequences for making a case for impact assessment. The question is, are administrators willing to release faculty from one course to do the kinds of research on program performance and outcomes that is needed to make a case for new resources?

Ultimately, five major internal constraints: process orientation, resistance to change, loss of romance, rigidification of decision-making, and loss of faculty partnerships, can only lead the community college on a course of decline in service and curriculum opportunities for students and community over the next two decades. Increasing competition for students and instability in funding, however, will surely shape the velocity with which change impacts the community colleges. And the degree to which a college is prepared to carefully examine these constraints and to respond to criticism, will partially determine the level of support they can expect to receive from funding sources, community agencies, students and taxpayers.

Embracing Vulnerabilities of Community Colleges

Community colleges have three vulnerabilities they will need to address by virtue of changing external conditions. Essentially these involve difficulties in the internal structure in conducting research on impact and outcomes. Community colleges would be severely impacted if financial stringency, perceptions of over-budgeting, and a decline in public perceptions were to become a reality. Alfred warns, "Unless colleges are prepared to document the impacts caused by a loss of financial support (or support that does not meet inflation) they are going to experience difficulty in sustaining the current level of resources. Moreover, a perception could develop that community colleges are over-budgeted. We do not talk too much about the benefits produced on a program-by-program basis and so what legislators see or what the public sees is only the cost factor - what it costs to operate the program without documentation of the benefit side of the equation. As a result, a decline in public perceptions about benefits to the student and to the community could arise when there is too much focus on costs and not enough attention to the relationship of benefits to the cost. Accountability to constituencies then becomes the medium of exchange in which *cost* and *value* is supported by groups both internal and external to the college.

Implications and Corrective Solutions for Community Colleges

Despite the significant number of internal and external factors and vulnerabilities which are confronting community colleges nationwide, efforts to gather impact information and data on student outcomes can meet with success if the community college today can take corrective action to improve their image both in the market of service providers and in their relationships with external constituencies.

The first step involves building a case for uniqueness in a way that it has not been built. For example, the low cost of tuition for students in this community college should be preserved. With the traditional prestige of the baccalaureate degree still intact, the community college must continue to deliver low-cost education to attract students. Otherwise students who may continue to prefer the four-year degree over the associate degree may choose to attend four-year colleges if tuition parity is achieved.

Relationships with public and private sector agencies, too, must be strengthened. Curricula need to be conceived more in terms of what business and industry need, not exclusively in terms of the needs of faculty and what they think should be taught. Consortia with other service providers and with public and private agencies can become an excellent method by which needs and solutions are communicated and understood.

Expansion and diversification of revenue sources should top the list of solutions as the consequences of not doing so will loom larger over community colleges in the future. The need to diversify funding sources can be met by involving business and industry and other private-sector sources in questions about the solvency of the college. The question is, can faculty and administrators rely on present funding sources or should they not expect industry to do more or the local tax district to do more? When looking at benefits offset to industry in terms of a trained labor pool stocked with well-prepared graduates, should not the community college receive, in turn, equipment, scholarships and other resources as a reward for meeting the manpower needs of the private sector?

In addition to achieving a win-win relationship with the private sector, attempts should be made to clarify and embellish the requirement for the associate degree, making the criteria and performance expectations clear and systematic. If the needs of business and industry continue to remain a priority concern, then establishing a uniform performance level for graduates may insure that recruiters and managers of private-sector organizations hold positive feelings about the reputation of the associate degree.

Whether it be decisions about uniqueness for the college or for looking at alternative funding sources, a fifth solution to help community colleges improve their situation is to eliminate the steps and time involved in the decision process. Too often, the college focuses on process and not outcomes. The elaborative, consultative networks that today clog the decision-making process is essentially creating an inefficient and ineffective way to operate the institution. The question remains, how fast can the college make a decision? Can it turn on a dime? And more importantly, how fast can the competition make a decision on the same items of consideration?

To be able to build a case for uniqueness for the community college requires a radically different approach to marketing the organization. Essentially this begins with marketing outcomes, not intentions. Students require different types of information as a support for attendance decisions today. They do not only want to know the courses that are being offered, they want to know the outcomes achieved by the students who take the courses. Institutions that begin to market the outcomes of what they produce as opposed to their intentions will have an advantage over other institutions. Ideally, this concept is the entire case for doing impact research. How can faculty and administrators market the college in the arena of providers so as to come out placing first in the competition? And are they doing the type of research that is going to give them comparative advantage over these competitors? One form of comparative advantage posed by Alfred that is particularly effective in making a case for community colleges is the principle of foregone earnings. He makes a case in point about the two-year student vs. the four-year student who asks, "For the amount of time I'm in school, how much income do I forego because I'm in school?" The example below can illustrate.

Two students start school, one in the community college and one in the university. It takes the two-year student two years, maybe two and a half, to get the associate degree. Over those two years he has paid $2,500 to get the degree. The cost is essentially minimum. Upon graduation, this person obtains a job paying $15,000 per year and over a four year time span has earned $30,000 with two years spent in direct employment. He has made a net income of $27,500 ($30,000 minus the $2,500 cost to obtain the associate degree). If this same student worked while attending school, his net gains would be even larger.

The four-year student, on the other hand, who has gone to school during this same span, earned nothing, went full time and paid $12,000 compared to the two-year community college student who by now has earned $27,500 and gained two year's work experience. The result for the four year student is a net of minus $12,000 without even hitting the job market.

Four years later the community college graduate now has his employer paying for the baccalaureate degree while still being fully employed during the following four years. And he has earned, for example, $72,000 while earning the baccalaureate simultaneously. The four year college student during this same time will have earned $20,000 per year for a total of $80,000.

When not even adding the employer benefits on top of what they have paid for tuition, after eight years the community college graduate with the baccalaureate degree has earned $99,500. The four-year graduate with the same baccalaureate degree has earned only $68,000 ($80,000 minus the $12,000 cost to obtain the baccalaureate degree). Both have the same degree, but the community college graduate has something else on his side—the job experience. He has two more years of experience at the lower level and is moving up the management hierarchy.

The key point in Alfred's scenario is that after eight years with both students having the same degree, the student holding the associate degree has earned more money and has more job experience. On the flip-side, the benefits in marketing this comparative advantage for the community college is to demonstrate to funding sources, potential student markets, the community and competing educational providers that there are *enormous cost-benefits for students* in terms of sheer bottom line impact.

Lastly, two additional corrective solutions are posed by Alfred regarding the internal constituency of the organization and a growing demand for leadership development within the community college system. He contends the structure of internal mangement will need to be shifted to produce a strong focus on institutional research compared to what now exists. Simply having a researcher on campus will not be enough to meet the developmental needs of the college.

Faculty will need to conduct research on the effects of their programs. This may entail releasing faculty from one course to allow them the time and opportunity to be a part of the research process. It is in the best interests of the college to utilize its academic resources to substantiate the outcomes of the learning process. One question remains: Are community colleges doing the types of institutional research that will provide them with a comparative advantage over competitors in the delivery of programs and quest for human and financial resources?

Leadership, without question, still remains one of the most essential ingredients of institutional vitality in the higher education market today. Innovative programs for leadership development can and will contribute greatly to the planning and decision-making of the future state of the community college system. "Opportunity with Excellence" cannot survive without opportunities for leadership renewal and for the development of new leaders in the community college today. The Presidents' Leadership Institute in North Carolina, the first of its kind for community college presidents, is a major case in point. With initiatives from other states and their legislatures, leadership programs in other states will emerge to provide the needed retooling for the presidential role that will be required to meet the demands of future citizens.

CONCLUSION

For the mid-level manager, the challenge through the year 2000 will not only be to help shape the mission of the college but to harness the resources that will build credibility into the outcomes of the institution. Strategic action rests significantly on the extent and nature of concepts and symbols available for orienting the participants (constituent groups) as well as the extent and nature of their communications both inside and outside the organization. Organizational leadership seeks to improve the satisfaction of participation and to increase the credibility of the organization in their eyes (Chaffee 1984).

Leaders' mission in building a case for uniqueness will be to clarify the image of the institution in the minds of the local and state constituency through impact research and its marketing. The label, Opportunity College, appropriately given to community colleges in the 1960's, can be redeclared in the name of excellence in the 1980s and '90s providing that commitment is driven towards low cost of tuition, building curricula for business and industry, redefining the associate degree, eliminating steps in the decision-making process, marketing outcomes, getting the faculty involved in the research process, and strengthening one's own leadership capabilities and those of the staff.

In making a case for community college impact studies as an adaptive strategy, Alfred shares this vision. Using institutional impact data provided to key decision-makers through an effective organization for institutional research, one can make the case for new resources. The question is, "Do we have the 'will' and conscience to undertake this task knowing full well that it may mean a fundamental change in our approach to management? I think the answer is 'yes' and I look to you to advance our colleges in the information society with a strategic organization for research" (Alfred 1983).

Reviewer for this Chapter

Pamela D. Grey
Staff Associate
Presidents' Leadership Institute and
    Associate Executive Director
National Council of Community
    College Business Officials
Department of Adult and
    Community College Education
North Carolina State University at
    Raleigh

REFERENCES

Alfred, R. L. "Impact Assessment: Making a Case for Community Colleges." Paper presented at the Presidents' Leadership Institute, Coastal Carolina Community College, Jacksonville, North Carolina, May 1984.

_____. "Socioeconomic Impact of Two-Year Colleges." In *ERIC Junior College Resource Review.* Los Angeles, California: ERIC Clearinghouse for Junior Colleges, March 1980: 1.

Breneman, D. W., and S. C. Nelson. *Financing Community Colleges: An Economic Perspective.* Washington, D.C.: The Brookings Institution, 1981: 200-201.

Chaffee, E. E. "Successful Strategic Management in Small Private Colleges." *Journal of Higher Education* 55, no. 2 (March/April 1984): 212-41.

Dunn, S. L. "The Changing University: Survival in the Information Society." *The Futurist* 17, no. 4, (August 1983): 55-60.

Ewell, P. *Information in Student Outcomes: How To Get It and How To Use It.* Boulder, Colorado: National Center for Higher Education Management Systems, 1983.

Gollattscheck, J. F. "Assessing Social and Economic Benefits to the Community." In *Institutional Impacts on Campus, Community and Business Constituencies.* New Directions for Community Colleges, no. 46. San Francisco: Jossey-Bass, 1982: 35-50.

_____. "Communicating to Constituencies in Terms They Can Understand and Support." Paper presented at the Presidents' Leadership Institute, Coastal Carolina Community College, Jacksonville, North Carolina, May 1984.

Koltai, L. (Chairman). *National Task Force to Redefine the Associate Degree: A Preliminary Presentation.* Washington, D.C.: American Association of Community and Junior Colleges, 1983: 87.

Melchiori, G. S., and N. Nash. "The Impact of Higher Education: An Analysis of the Research." Paper presented at the National Forum of the Association for Institutional Research, Toronto, Canada, 1983.

Myran, G. A. (ed.) *Strategic Management in the Community Colleges* New Directions for Community Colleges, no. 44. San Francisco: Jossey-Bass, 1983.

Palmer, J. C. "How is Quality Measured at the Community College? *Community College Review* 11, no. 3 (Winter 1983-84): 52-61.

Parnell, D. "Opportunity with Excellence: Vision of the Future." Interview by Dale F. Campbell and Robert M. Stivender, 13 June 1984. Tape recording, American Association of Community and Junior Colleges, Washington, D.C.

Wattenbarger, J. I. "The Dilemma of Reduced Resources: Action or Reaction?" In *Coping with Reduced Resources.* New Directions for Community Colleges, no. 22. San Francisco: Jossey-Bass, 1978: 61-65.

Young, J. E. "A Study to Determine Variables Associated with Success of Selected Florida Public Two-Year Community Junior Colleges in Obtaining Categorical Aid Funds from the Federal Government." Ph.D., University of Florida, 1977.

Conclusion

CHALLENGES, ADAPTIVE STRATEGIES AND COMPETENCIES FOR THE FUTURE

Dale F. Campbell

In selecting the objectives for the institute a decision was made that learning some lessons from research on another segment of higher education—small private colleges—might be particularly beneficial at this juncture in the history of the movement. With what has been called the deregulation of higher education, these institutions have by economic necessity either adapted or died. Many adaptive strategies reviewed in this volume were first utilized in small private colleges (i.e. public relations, resource development, recruiting and marketing, etc.).

What are the major trends impacting your college that you can do something about? What strategies were found to make a difference in addressing these trends? And finally, what new competencies will be required of you as leaders? A synthesis of the selected institute outcomes points to these four core findings:

CHALLENGE - Rapid Technological Developments. George Keller states that the new computer and communications technology is transforming the traditional art of teaching and the entire nature of educational delivery. In 1984, Japan introduced its "broadcast" university which utilized public television to deliver a range of collegiate courses to the general Japanese public. The technology is in place today to create the All American University in which the most distinguished faculty in all fields would reside and prepare instructional programs for satellite transmission across the nation.

ADAPTIVE STRATEGY - Human Resource Development. Dale Campbell states that with cost so prohibitive in the area of high cost, soon to be obsolete equipment, priorities in funding occupational education must shift to the faculties' acquisition of new knowlege. Staff development could be the most critical resource if redefined to focus on computer literacy, formation of information networks, cooperative education, contracting and topics which focus on the faculty role as resource person and facilitator of learning.

Jim Hammons states that "there is not any one thing as important to institutions and to the future of them than people, and, what we do in terms of selecting people, placing them on the job, orienting them, developing them, the way we utilize our personnel, and then the way we evaluate and hopefully as a consequence of that, reward them. There's no other aspect of our institution, in my

117

opinion, that is as important as that." Personnel development must be continuous and intentional.

NEW COMPETENCIES
- Mangement of change.
- Ability to use technology to optimize performance.
- Develop and administer accurate and meaningful programs of faculty evaluation and development.

CHALLENGE - Changing Economy.

In shifting from an industrial to an information-service economy, Keller predicts that the costs of education will increase faster than other sectors of the economy. Education will continue to remain a labor intensive endeavor, not lending itself to increases in productivity. With increasing demands on public revenues, the public and funding sources will demand cost reductions and increased productivity resulting in future political concerns for education leaders.

ADAPTIVE STRATEGY - Resource Development and Marketing.

Richard Alfred states that aggressive strategies for resource development and reallocation will be needed to produce discretionary income for program development. Administrators who allow weak and ineffective programs to consume vital resources, weaken the entire fabric of the organization. New strategies for marketing college programs should be developed with a focus on research and student outcomes, social and economic impacts and cost-benefits. Focus should be marketing the outcome of our product - learning—not institutional intentions.

NEW COMPETENCIES
- Fund raising.
- Marketing.
- Creative management of finances.
- Research -trend analyses, assessing needs impact assessment, evaluation of outcomes which focus on our product.

CHALLENGE - Increasing Competition.

According to Keller the higher education monopoly on adult educatioon has been relinguished to a growing plethora of institutions and agencies which have vested interest in adult development. Today one out of every six museums offers college courses. Private business spends over $14 billion annually on employee development. Many corporations have actually begun the operation of company colleges awarding both undergraduate and graduate degrees in the technologies. The armed services continue to provide the bulk of much of the nation's technical training. Over 50% of the electronic technicians now serving the private sector received their training in the military.

Competition for shrinking dollars has made it imperative for all public institutions to be able to prove a form of uniqueness and demonstrate their value to taxpayers when legislators begin to favor other service providers.

ADAPTIVE STRATEGY - Focus the Curriculum.

One must realize, according to Parnell, that community colleges are not the only providers of services to the communities. Linkages will be the name of the game for the next 15 years . . . linkages with business and industry to further cooperative education programs; linkages with high schools and 4-year institutions to create closer articulation of the programs which precede and follow those of the community college; linkages with community-based human service organizations to increase support of adult education. The community college leaders who survive will be those who choose to cooperate rather than do combat with other providers.

In studying attempts by selected private colleges to deal with decline, Ellen Chaffee identifies two strategic models. The first is the adaptive model, which involves attuning the organization to changes in market demands. The second strategy discussed by Chaffee is the interpretive model, which accepts that an organization is a network of individuals; and a key leadership role is to assure the management of meaning or focus on mission. There was not a "new program-needed mentality" in an effort to attract students. Rather, marginal changes, not major changes, were made in the curriculum programs. Institutions did not pursue new missions that were outside the expertise of the faculty. Business and academics were not allowed to function separately. The successful colleges in Chaffee's study were those that found their own unique blend of the adaptive and the interpretive. Administrators should use an interpretive model of strategy in assessing the needs of their constituents. When a proposal for a new high-demand program is presented, the program must be integral to the institution's mission. Hence, curriculum grows out of mission.

John Roueche states that leadership is caring about the quality of the institution. One must behave as though he really cares about what goes on in the organization. If one doesn't care about the quality of the enterprise it will not happen. Mediocrity will be the end result. Having expectations for the faculty and students shows care. Signaling expectations (caring) may be as simple as asking the right questions such as, "Is anyone learning anything around here?" What can be done in an educational institution is powerful if one expects something to happen and asks key pivotal questions.

NEW COMPETENCIES
- Master politician.
- Establishing linkages.
- Focus on mission in decision making.
- Caring - asking the right questions.
- Motivating - developing and maintaining high standards and clear performance objectives.

CHALLENGE - Questioning Identity.

Leadership for the movement has been in transition and so has the movement's identity. In fact Campbell's "new challenges for leadership" article might have been titled more aptly "New Leaders for the Challenge." The past few years have seen a number of significant changes in the character of the leadership of the movement with its passing of the mantle to leaders in a new era: nationally from what Vaughan calls Edmund Gleazer, Jr., the philosopher, to Dale Parnell, the pragmatist; in North Carolina from Larry Blake, the formalizer, to Bob Scott, the politician. Each man seemingly is right for his time—history will ultimately judge. George Vaughan states that "the community college is facing a crisis of identity that may prove to be as significant as any other event in its development." With the shift in leadership it is only natural to have some loss of identity and cohesiveness. Richard Alfred argues that a case must be made for uniqueness; or becoming a redundant organization in higher education will be the risk.

ADAPTIVE STRATEGY - Creative Leadership and Governance.

Ben Lawrence cites Chaffee's recent National Center for Higher Education Management Systems research which concludes that adaptive strategies alone do not turn around declining colleges. Rather ". . . these schools were led by people who sought to construct reality in accordance with their perceptions of what the organization ought to be . . . They established and maintained a strong, and clear sense of organizational identity—and they made major decisions on the basis of that identitiy." Her conclusion merits quoting for your reflection on its applicability to your institution where the leader's principal role emerges as that of teacher, conveyor of our philosophy, the "manager of meaning." She concludes with a powerful statement that ". . . sincerity, diligence, and even sophisticated analyses of demand cannot overcome the absence of a shared perception of what the college is about and why it matters or a shared conviction that it is capable of making good on its promises."

COMPETENCIES

- Commitment to clear vision and mission of the comprehensive open-door philosophy—extending opportunity with excellence.
- Ability to plan strategically.
- Integrating left and right brain skills.
- Work with and through trustees.
- Clarify image.
- Teacher.
- Commitment to professionalizing the mangement team.

Dale Parnell emphasizes the importance of tomorrow's leaders also being teachers. "If, in fact, our major product is learning, then everything we do should support learning in the institution . . . I would like to see all of the leadership programs . . . aim at the central core of our product and that's learning, the understanding of learning, and being supportive of that."

THE ULTIMATE CHALLENGE

These then are some of the major trends impacting community colleges today. Regardless of whether you view them as threats or as opportunities, they are clearly challenges for leadership which must be met.

Perhaps what is needed most in this stage of development of the community college movement is to re-examine its roots, adapt our institutions to these challenges in the context of mission, and with a clear vision rededicate ourselves to making good on the promise of the national slogan, "achieving opportunity with excellence." To that end this volume concludes with two men's visions of the community college—one a founding father of a system, the other the chief national advocate of community, technical and junior colleges.

Dr. Dallas W. Herring, former Chairman, State Board of Education, North Carolina Community College System, challenges us to "rededicate ourselves to the philosophy of total education." Exercepts from his address are reprinted in Appendix E. Fryer states that in developing leaders "the most important set of assumptions that any administrator holds has to do with his or her beliefs concerning the nature of human beings . . . to become consciously aware of their basic beliefs and values."[1] Herring eloquently seeks to rekindle our commitment to extending the right of every man and woman to develop to their fullest ability." He calls on us to rededicate ourselves to the hallmark of the community college philosophy and mission—that of extending access to all who may profit from instruction.

Secondly, Dr. Dale Parnell, President, American Association of Community and Junior Colleges and chief national spokesperson of the movement, shares with us in Appendix F his visions for the future of the community college. He states that "If we fail to develop leaders with the competencies to not only see our new frontiers but deal with them effectively, I think we're going to . . . stall in the ability to serve the needs of our citizens as lifelong learners." Community colleges have historically been noted for their ability to adapt in response to the changes in society and the resulting needs of the constituencies they serve. Unquestionably these are challenging times as are those that befall each generation of leaders. You are challenged to further explore the implications of these strategies for yourself and your institution. The key adaptive strategies of human resource development, resource development and marketing, and focusing the curriculum, coupled with creative leadership, can form the foundation for the new management style for community colleges. Hopefully this volume has stimulated your thinking, provided an initial foundation for rekindling your spirit to rededicate yourself with vigor to achieving the unique mission of your institution.

---

[1] Thomas W. Fryer, Jr. "Developing Leaders Through Graduate Education." In *Emerging Roles for Community College Leaders*, no. 46. San Francisco: Jossey-Bass, Inc. 1984: 102.

Appendix A

ADAPTIVE STRATEGIES AND LEADERSHIP COMPETENCIES FOR A NEW ERA

Competency Diagnostic Assessment

The main objective of this assessment is to assist you in determining your professional education needs as a community college administrator as measured by the difference between your perceptions of your current level of expertise in certain competencies and what you perceive that level should be.

Indicate on the 7-point scale in the first column the perceived level of your *present* competency identified. Then on the 7-point scale in the second column, indicate the level of competency you feel you should possess to execute your present job responsibilities in the identified competency. Indicate your choices by *circling* the appropriate number on each scale.

Challenge	*Adaptive Strategy*
Rapid Technological Developments (See Keller, Ch. 1; Bender, Ch. 5)	Human Resource Development (See Hammons & Hudgins, Ch. 4; Bender & Anderson, Ch. 5)
Changing Economy (See Keller, Ch. 1; Vaughan, Ch. 2)	Resource Development and Marketing (See Keener & Blong, Ch. 6; Alfred, Ch. 7)
Increasing Competition (See Keller, Ch. 1; Vaughan, Ch. 2; Alfred, Ch. 7)	Focusing the Curriculum (See Roueche & Barton, Ch. 3; Richardson & Vaughan, Ch. 2)
Changing Identify (See Vaughan, Ch. 2; Alfred, Ch. 7)	Creative Leadership and Governance (See Keller & McClenney, Ch. 1; Richardson & Vaughan, Ch. 2; Roueche & Barton, Ch. 3; Hammons & Hudgins, Ch. 4; Alfred, Ch. 7; Campbell, Conclusion)

0	1	2	3	4	5	6
Absent			Moderate (conceptual understanding)			High (expert)

Competency	Present	Needed
• Managing change	0 1 2 3 4 5 6	0 1 2 3 4 5 6
• Using technology to optimize performance	0 1 2 3 4 5 6	0 1 2 3 4 5 6
• Administering valid faculty development and evaluation programs	0 1 2 3 4 5 6	0 1 2 3 4 5 6
• Fund raising	0 1 2 3 4 5 6	0 1 2 3 4 5 6
• Marketing	0 1 2 3 4 5 6	0 1 2 3 4 5 6
• Managing finances creatively	0 1 2 3 4 5 6	0 1 2 3 4 5 6
• Analyzing research trends, assessing impact, evaluating outcomes	0 1 2 3 4 5 6	0 1 2 3 4 5 6
• Being a master politician	0 1 2 3 4 5 6	0 1 2 3 4 5 6
• Establishing linkages	0 1 2 3 4 5 6	0 1 2 3 4 5 6
• Focusing on mission in decision-making	0 1 2 3 4 5 6	0 1 2 3 4 5 6
• Caring about quality of the enterprise	0 1 2 3 4 5 6	0 1 2 3 4 5 6
• Motivating others by developing and maintaining high standards and clear performance objectives	0 1 2 3 4 5 6	0 1 2 3 4 5 6
• Committing to the mission—extending opportunity with excellence	0 1 2 3 4 5 6	0 1 2 3 4 5 6
• Planning strategically	0 1 2 3 4 5 6	0 1 2 3 4 5 6
• Integrating left and right brain skills	0 1 2 3 4 5 6	0 1 2 3 4 5 6
• Working with and through trustees	0 1 2 3 4 5 6	0 1 2 3 4 5 6
• Clarifying the image	0 1 2 3 4 5 6	0 1 2 3 4 5 6
• Teaching	0 1 2 3 4 5 6	0 1 2 3 4 5 6
• Committing to professionalization of the management team	0 1 2 3 4 5 6	0 1 2 3 4 5 6

Appendix B

MINTZBERG'S TEN ROLES

1. *Interpersonal Roles*
   a) Figurehead - carries out social, inspirational, legal and ceremonial duties as a function of status.
   b) Leader - considers needs of organization and its members in developing a climate conducive to effectiveness; motivates, supervises, hires, trains and promotes.
   c) Liaison - works with people outside the organization to manage boundary conditions and ensure access to needed resources.

2. *Informational Roles*
   d) Monitor - seeks and receives information from inside and outside the organization - develops his/her own information system.
   e) Disseminator - transmits internal and external information about facts and values relevant to institutional mission to subordinates. (Selective transmission determines relative openness of communication).
   f) Spokesman - transmits information to individuals outside the organization - public information and legislative liaison activities are included.

3. *Decisional Roles*
   g) Entrepreneur - initiation and design of controlled changed within the organization.
   h) Disturbance Handler - deals with conflict produced by change as well as any situation for which the organization has no programmed response (and hence, must depend on managerial judgment).
   i) Resource Allocator - maintains control of strategic processes by authorizing implementation of decisions.
   j) Negotiator - takes charge when his/her organization must enter into agreements or resolve differences with another organization.

(Mintzberg, 1973)

Summation of Mintzberg's TEN ROLES OF MANAGEMENT from *The Nature of Managerial Work* by Henry Mintzberg.
Copyright © 1973 by Henry Mintzberg
Reprinted by permission of Harper & Row, Publishers, Inc.

Appendix C

OCCUPATIONAL PROGRAM COMPONENTS OF COOPERATIVE EDUCATION

Three new courses were developed to attain the desired occupational program competency levels. Which courses were taken was dependent upon the student's prior experience and individual career goals.

Occupational Program Components of Cooperative Education

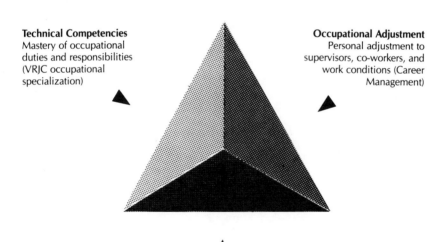

Technical Competencies
Mastery of occupational duties and responsibilities (VRJC occupational specialization)

Occupational Adjustment
Personal adjustment to supervisors, co-workers, and work conditions (Career Management)

Career Development Competencies
Continuous testing and adjustments to career goals (Career Development)

1. Career Development Competencies for career exploration and decisionmaking — Human Development H.D. 301. Career Development (3-0)

    Designed for persons interested in developing positive educational/career choices through individual and group exploration. Students may expect to work through various assignments and exercises to increase interactions with others and awareness to self.

    Staffed primarily by Student Services approved vocational counselors and targeted for the undecided major.

2. Occupational Adjustment — Supervisory Management S.Man. 303. Career Management (3-0)

    Personal adjustment to supervisors, co-workers, and work conditions. Includes the study of job seeking, job getting, and job keeping skills.

    Staffed by approved Mid-Management faculty or proposed Cooperative Education Coordinator and targeted for declared majors with no prior work experience.

3. Supervised Work Experience/Cooperative Education — Example of Building Construction Technology BCT 441, 442, 443. Cooperative Education Seminar and Work Experience (320 clock hours)

    A comprehensive treatment of internship related activities, individualized objectives, and regularly scheduled seminars related to the student's occupational specialization. Student will spend a minimum of 20 hours per week at an approved job while enrolled in each of the courses. Prerequisite: S. Man. 303 or consent of instructor.

    Staffed by approved faculty in student's occupational specialization and provides a built-in mechanism to award credit for prior work experience. (Vernon Regional Junior College 1980)

(Rippy and Campbell 1982)

Appendix D

ESSENTIAL PUBLICATIONS AND HELPFUL AGENCIES FOR DEVELOPMENT OFFICERS

FEDERAL PUBLICATION AND AGENCY INFORMATION

AMERICAN EDUCATION

U.S. Government Printing Office
Superintendent of Documents
Washington, D.C. 20402 (202) 275-2051
Published: Bi-Monthly

CATALOG OF FEDERAL DOMESTIC ASSISTANCE

U.S. Government Printing Office
Superintendent of Documents
Washington, D.C. 20402 (202) 275-2051
Published: annually

THE CHRONICLE OF HIGHER EDUCATION

P.O. Box 1965
Marion, Ohio 43305 (614) 383-3141
Published: Weekly

FEDERAL GRANTS MANAGEMENT HANDBOOK & CHAPTERS

Grants Management Advisory Service
1725 K Street N.W. Suite 200
Washington, D.C. 2006 (202) 872-1776
Published: Periodic Up-dates

FEDERAL REGISTER

U.S. Government Printing Office
Superintendent of Documents
Washington, D.C. 20402
Published: Daily Mon-Fri

FEDERAL RESEARCH REPORT

951 Pershing Drive
Silver Spring, MD 20910 (301) 587-6300
Published: Weekly

FEDERAL YELLOW BOOK

Washington Monitor
Suite 449
National Press Building
Washington, D.C. 20045 (202) 347-7757
Published: Periodic Up-dates

GRANTS & AID TO INDIVIDUALS IN THE ARTS

Washington International Arts Letter
Box 9005
Washington, D.C. 20003 (212) 246-4510
Published: Annually

GUIDE TO FEDERAL ASSISTANCE VOL. 1 & 2

Wellborn Associates, Inc.
5781 Beaumont Avenue
La Jolla, CA 92037 (619) 454-1412
Published: Annually with Monthly Up-dates

HEALTH PLANNING MANPOWER	Capitol Publications Inc. 1330 North 17th Street Arlington, Virginia 22009 (703) 528-5400
HIGHER EDUCATION *NATIONAL AFFAIRS NEWSLETTER*	American Council on Education 1 Dupont Circle Suite 800 Washington, D.C. 20036-1193 (202) 293-7050 Published: Bi-Weekly
HUMANITIES	Superintendent of Documents U.S. Government Printing Office Washington, D.C. 20402 (202) 275-2051 Published: Bi-Monthly
KIPLINGER WASHINGTON LETTER	1729 H. Street N. W. Washington, D.C. 20006 (202) 887-6400 Published: Weekly
VOCATIONAL TRAINING NEWS	Capitol Publications, Inc. 1330 North 17th Street Arlington, Virginia 22009 (703) 528-5400 Published: Weekly
THE ESTATE ANALYST	Kennedy Sinclaire 524 Hamburg Turnpike P.O. Box 34 Wayne, NJ 07470 (201) 942-2000 Published: Periodically

PRIVATE PUBLICATION AND AGENCY INFORMATION

COUNCIL FOR ADVANCEMENT AND *SUPPORT OF EDUCATION (CASE)*	Associate Vice President Independent Schools CASE Suite 400, 11 Dupont Circle Washington, D.C. 20036 (202) 328-5954
DESIGNS FOR FUND-RAISING	By Harold J. Seymour. Contact your local bookstore. ISBN 0-07-056356-3
THE ESTATE ANALYST	Kennedy Sinclaire 524 Hamburg Turnpike P.O. Box 34 Wayne, N.J. 07470 (201) 942-2000
THE FOUNDATION CENTER	888 Seventh Avenue New York, N. Y. 10106 (800) 424-9836
FOUNDATION NEWS	1828 L Street N. W. Washington, D.C. 20036 (800) 424-9836 Published: Bi-Monthly
FUND-RAISING INSTITUTE	Box 365 Amber, PA 19002-0365 (215) 646-7019
FUND-RAISING COUNCIL	500 Fifth Avenue, Suite 1015 New York, NY 10036
GONSER, GERBER, TINKER, *STUHR ON DEVELOPMENT*	105 West Madison Chicago, IL 60602
THE GRANTSMANSHIP CENTER	1031 S. Grand Avenue Los Angeles, CA 90015 (213) 749-4721
HARVARD BUSINESS REVIEW	Subscription Service Department P.O. Box 4040 Woburn, MA 01888 Published: Monthly

HOW TO BUILD A BIG ENDOWMENT	Public Mangement Institute 333 Hayes Street San Francisco, CA 94102 (415) 896-1900
ORYX PRESS	2214 North Central Avenue, Suite 103 Phoenix, AZ 85004
THE NONPROFIT EXECUTIVE	Taft 5125 MacArthur Boulevard, N.W. Washington, D.C. 20016 (202) 966-7086 Published: Monthly
NONPROFIT CORPORATIONS, *ORGANIZATIONS & ASSOCIATIONS* *by Howard L. Oleck*	Prentice-Hall In. Book Distribution Center Route 59 at Brook Hill Drive West Nyack, New York 10895 (914) 358-8800
PHILANTHROPY & MARKETING *NEW STRATEGIES FOR FUND RAISING* *by James Gregory Lord*	Third Sector Press P.O. Box 18044 Cleveland, OH 44118 (216) 932-6066
THE PHILANTHROPY MONTHLY	P. O. Box 989 New Milford, Conn. 06776 (203) 354-7132 Published: Monthly
TAFT FOUNDATION REPORTER *(Annually); FOUNDATION UPDATES* *(Monthly); FOUNDATION GIVING* *WATCH (Bi-Monthly)*	Taft Foundation Information System 5125 MacArthur Boulevard, N.W. Washington, D.C. 20016 (202) 966-7086

NATIONAL COUNCIL FOR RESOURCE DEVELOPMENT

Affiliate of the American Association of Community and Junior Colleges

Copies of NCRD Reprints and reference book may be obtained by writing:
NCRD
Suite 410, One Dupont Circle, N.W.
Washington, D.C. 20036-1176 (202) 293-7050

Principal Reference Handbook:
Sharron, H.W., Jr.(ed) *The Community College Foundation* Washington, D.C.:
National Council for Resource Development, 1982.

NCRD RESOURCE PAPERS

1. Resource Development Concept: Institutional Resources. Joyce Smitheran, 1973
2. Funding Sources for Community Services: The State and Local Community. Harvey Sharron, Jr. 1974
3. Federal Relations in Community and Junior Colleges. Jack Orcutt, 1974
4. How to be Successful at Grantsmanship, Guidelines for Proposal Writing Generalization: Foundation Proposal. Dr. Barbara Young, 1980
5. A Federal Glossary. Lowell Cook, 1975
6. Special Projects. Sanford Schneider
7. The Role of the Professional Educator as the College Development Officer. Dr. James L. Wattenbarger, 1976
8. Profiles of Federal Programs Administrators in Multi-Unit Community Colleges. Anthony D. Calabro, 1976
9. The Small College and Federal Funding. Dr. Bonny Franke
10. Government Relations in Community and Junior Colleges: Some Perspectives. Dr. Robert J. Leo, 1976

11. Higher Education in the Age of the Economist and Consumer. Carmelo L. Battaglia, 1976.
12. Indirect Costs: An Introduction for the Community College Development Officer. Dr. Judson H. Flower, 1976
13. The IPA-An Opportunity for Intergovernmental Understanding. Dr. Christine E. Anderson, 1977
14. Opportunities for Improving Science Education Using National Science Foundation Grants. Malcolm Goldberg, 1977
15. Conditions and Factors Associated with Successful Federal Funding. Dr. John E. Young, 1978
16. National Endowment for the Arts: What's In It For Community Colleges Ginger Hoffland, 1978
17. Winning Foundation and Corporate Grants Christine M. Van Ness, 1978
18. The Development and Organization of the Community College Foundation. W. Harvey Sharron, Jr., 1978
19. Fundamentals of Writing a Grants Proposal. Dr. James H. Young, 1979
20. Predictable Crises in Resource Development. Richard J. Jackson, 1979
21. The CETA Amendments of 1978 - How They Relate to the Two Year Educational Institution. Dennis Linderbaum, 1979
22. Federal Support for Higher Education: A Look Ahead. Shirley H. Woodie, 1979
23. Characteristics and Conditions of a Successful Community College Foundation. Edward F. Duffy, 1980
24. The Role of the College President in Resource Development. Richard Mosier, 1980
25. The Education Division General Administration Regulations and the Implications for Resource Development. W. Harvey Sharron, Jr., 1980
26. The Coming Changes In Our School System. Peter F. Drucker, u.d.
27. The Federal Contract Process "An Untapped Resource for Community Colleges." Frank G. Adams, u.d.
28. Resource Development Through Consortium Approach. Dr. Phillip Petray, u.d.

Special Reprint: The Resource Development Officer. Dr. R. David Hodge, u.d.

Appendix E

A REDEDICATION OF THE PHILOSOPHY TO TOTAL EDUCATION

W. Dallas Herring

Our policies must not assume that technicians and skilled workers are automatons incapable of human aspiration and achievement. Education for employment is essential for them, but it is not enough. They also are human beings and citizens with immense potential for good.

There are still those among us who, fancying themselves above anything resembling manual labor, will encourage the notion that education for work is somehow beneath the dignity of a class whose forebears earned them their place in society by honest manual labor of which incidentally, they were not ashamed. These are outworn notions which must be overcome. They are unworthy of honorable men, for they subvert the ends of justice in a society which itself represents the ultimate in diversity of both interest and ability.

It is either a false idea, or else one which is too abstruse for me, that one cannot be both a philosopher and a workman made worthy of his hire through education and more worthy of his citizenship through familiarity with the great ideas that moved western civilization ahead. Every man is to some extent a philosopher. Democracy makes that assumption. It risks its very existence on that assumption. If we do not really believe this, how can we risk letting him in the voting places where so much of our future is decided?

To every man belongs the right, as Thomas Wolfe said, "to become whatever his manhood and his vision can combine to make." Who is it with wisdom so great and with power so vast over the lives of men, that he can decide as a matter of public policy that mechanics need not appreciate beauty, that day laborers do not need to know very profoundly the difference between right and wrong or that ladies and gentleman of culture and good breeding should, by inference, consider work beneath them? This is the kind of decision which no one has a right to make for others in a free state, for the state must not discriminate. The state must be fair. It must be equitable in the provisions it makes for the benefit of all of its citizens. Those who propose its policies, and those who implement them, must see to it that these ends are served: that the vision and the manhood of all North Carolinians have the freedom to combine in the pursuit of many excellent things, each of which is worthy of our respect, if not in every case our admiration.

So let us climb "the mountains of tradition!" Let us "move forward while we may," as our new State President said when he brought about great change in the State's system of higher education as Governor. Where there are those who cannot read, let us teach them to read, for it is the key to all learning. Where there are those who did not graduate from high school, let us provide them with opportunity for a high school education and award them their diplomas when they earn them. That may seem to some traditionalists to be stooping very low to conquer ignorance, but is it a better thing that ignorance be left unconquered? Let us train and educate the technicians and never forget that they are also human beings with immense capability for good when they have the opportunity to learn also in the arts that befit free men.

One of the Hebrew prophets summed up the ideals of the educated man when he said, simply, "Do good, and not evil." He did not say, in a passive way, that one should strive to be good and to refrain from being evil. There is a vast amount of difference between being good and doing good. In order for one to do good in society he must have the ability to make choices of great character and insight. The most dangerous of men are those who are given to action without thought, but the most disappointing are those who think and do not act. It is the ideal of North Carolina that through universal education, through total education, through education which will enable all of its citizens both to reason and to do, the great society will one day be achieved. Let us now rededicate the communioty college system, without apology, stoutly and with good heart, to that end.

Editor's Note: This is an excerpt of Dr. Herring's keynote address to the North Carolina Community College Adult Educators' Association conference, Raleigh, N. C., May 5, 1983 commemorating the Twentieth Anniversary of the North Carolina Community College System.

W. Dallas Herring is a former Chairman of the North Carolina State Board of Education and is presently a member of the Editorial *Community College Review*. He is recognized as the father of the state's two-year community and technical colleges and was a recipient of the State Board of Community Colleges Twentieth Anniversary Awards.

Reprinted with permission *Community College Review*.

Appendix F

DALE PARNELL'S VISIONS FOR THE FUTURE

Successful colleges are led by people who establish a strong, clear organizational identity and mission, make decisions on that identity, and convey that mission to others. Perhaps it's time to dedicate yourself to establishing and conveying the unique mission of your institution. What are your visions of the future for your community college?

One man who has some well-defined visions for the movement as a whole is Dr. Dale Parnell, President and Chief Executive Officer, American Association of Community and Junior Colleges:

My first vision is that the associate degree will become the preferred degree for the hiring of technicians; I'm talking about that whole range of midlevel jobs that are increasing in volume in this country, that do not require a baccalaureate degree but require some education and training beyond high school.

Secondly, my vision is that we will have developed better and more closely articulated programs with the high schools. We have been working on something we are calling a "two-plus-two" associate degree, an associate degree that is really a four-year program that starts with the junior year in high school.

Third, my vision is that we could have a better relationship with the four-year colleges and universities of this country. I would like to see our college transfer program be so strong that there would be automatic transfer of credits from our institutions to the universities, without question.

I would like to see us tripled and quadrupled in the number of women and minority role model leaders in our institutions, whether that be women presidents, black presidents, Hispanic presidents, deans, or trustees.

I have another little vision: I hope that the president of the United States will be a community college graduate by the year 2000. I hope that leaders in business and industry, congressmen, state legislators, governors, etc., will be community college graduates and will proudly list that fact on their resume.

I would like to see as a part of the foreign policy of our country, the notion that community, technical and junior colleges are a resource and it is an exportable American idea in helping Third World countries, particularly to develop the technician class, the middle class for their nation.

I also have a vision that the community college faculty will view the community college as the premier teaching assignments in higher education—that the highest and best virtue that they could achieve in their life would be to teach in a community college.

I would love to see our leadership training programs aim at this idea of helping current leaders as well as incoming leaders to develop their competencies . . . and for this to be the norm for leadership for us throughout the country (Parnell, 1984).

133

Appendix G

EVALUATION OF PRESIDENTS' LEADERSHIP INSTITUTE AS A PILOT PROJECT

INTRODUCTION

The Presidents' Leadership Institute was funded as a pilot project to in part determine the feasibility of the design as a model for leadership development.

The primary goal of the project was to provide chief executive officers in the North Carolina community college systems an opportunity to experience practical applications and theoretical study of proven techniques and strategies for leadership in the emerging high-technology, information society. Acquiring new skills and sharing in current research would, over time, help presidents develop new competencies as leaders in order to build stronger linkages with faculty, their legislature, community and student body. Moreover, this goal supports and further clarifys Dale Parnell's vision for the future. "Leaders," he states, "must possess the ability to clarify the values of the organization and to structure their institutions to bring out the best in people."

Thirty eight presidents from the fifty eight colleges initially participated in the seven planned Institute sessions. From this, twenty one presidents applied to the Institute for graduation upon completion of the pilot project in May of 1983. Seventeen presidents received certificates of participation having attended 3 or more of the planned sessions. Four presidents received certificates of excellence for more intensive study which involved participation in 3 or more Institute sessions, completion of a case study, and final presentation of an exemplary program from their respective institutions at the final Institute session in May. After having completed the seven planned Institutes during the course of the 1983-1984 year it is clear, as evidenced in the reports back from presidential participants, that the Institute has some significant strengths as a model program for leadership development.

Institute Outcomes

Over the course of 8 months, 7 planned sessions took place at individual host campuses across the state of North Carolina. Sessions were strategically located to cover both urban and rural settings, making host campuses more easily accessible to those presidents located in either the far eastern or western parts of the state.

Upon completion of each session, attending presidents received a formative evaluation which asked them to identify significant outcomes which have been the result of their exposure to the last Institute attended. The following is a review of the formative evaluation itself, and the feedback received from presidents over the course of the 7 sessions.

The formative evaluation was mailed to each president within 30 days after their attendance to an Institute. It was developed to initiate personal responses to impressions gained, information processed, and actions taken by these individuals as a result of an Institute session. The individual responses then became a way to track the actual outcomes perceived or realized by everyone, providing a means to assess if collective or like outcomes occurred.

The Formative Evaluation

The evaluation form itself was composed of 7 questions, each asking the participant to rate or explain a perceived outcome or an actual response they had undertaken as a result of the information received from the guest consultants from the prior Institute. Moreover, impressions, favorable or unfavorable, and recommended suggestions to improve future Institute sessions were requested. This aided the Institute staff in the planning and implementation of future sessions, insuring that problems be minimized or eliminated.

In making an assessment of the evaluations, the most striking outcomes came from comparing responses to each question across all seven Institutes. Although it is important to look at each Institute session individually, for the purpose of assessing outcomes of the Institute as a whole, reviewing responses across the board resulted in findings which led to some uniformity in decision-making - outcomes which demonstrated group trends. The results of these evaluations will be described below, question by question, with particular emphasis being placed on group outcomes and ranked responses which predominately received the greatest attention.

Question No. 1 was an assessment of the individual's own competency in the subject matter (i.e., computers and information systems or resource development and marketing) before and after an Institute. Figure 1. represents the question and the rating scale that was used.

Figure 1

Question (1) in Formative Evaluation

1. Indicate your perceived level of competency in the subject matter of the last Institute session you attended by *circling* appropriate number on scales.

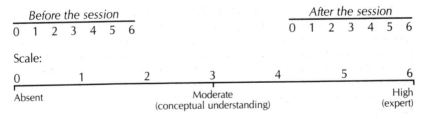

On the scale of 0 through 6, most participants first rated themselves at the "moderate conceptual understanding" level, number 3. Some rated themselves number 2, but no one rated themselves zero or having no competency in the subject matter. Alternately in the ratings for after the sessions, no one rated themselves "high or expert" in the sessions. At most, participants moved two levels upward with the majority of responses taking a one level increase in competency level.

Question no. 2 asked respondents to indicate the degree to which they felt favorable or unfavorable about their experience with consultants' sessions. Figure 2 represents the question and the rating scale that was used.

Figure 2

Question (2) in Formative Evaluation

2. Indicate the degree to which you feel favorable or unfavorable about your experience with the subject matter/book(s)/articles you were exposed to during the last Institute session you attended. Indicate choices by *circling* the appropriate number.

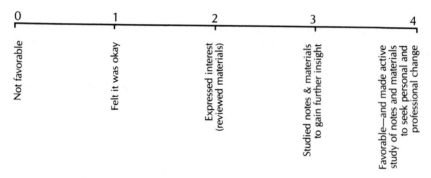

The response to this question which rated the participant's receptiveness to the session resulted in mixed reactions. No one stated they were "not favorable" to a session, however, most sessions received a combination of two's, three's, and fours. Only one Institute received an almost unanimous rating of "four" and this was the February Institute on Human Resource Development.

Question no. 3, without question, had the most uniform responses than any question asked in the formative evaluation. Question no. 3 asked the participants to indicate those groups of associates with which they shared their information and or materials with from the preceeding Institute. And participants were asked to rate the degree to which these were shared with one or more of the ten associated groups that were listed. Figure 3 represents the question and the rating scale that was used.

The responses to this question from the participant when indicating the groups in which information or materials were shared narrowed quickly down to three primary groups: other attending presidents; management councils, and staff. Sharing with faculty members, number 7. on the list was the fourth most often

Figure 3

Question (3) in Formative Evaluation

3. Indicate by circling appropriate number, the group(s) you have shared information with since attending the last Institute. Also, indicate the degree to which information on subject matter was shared by circling appropriate number.

1.	Other attending presidents	0 1 2 3 4 5 6
2.	Presidents who did not attend	0 1 2 3 4 5 6
3.	Management Council	0 1 2 3 4 5 6
4.	Board of Trustees	0 1 2 3 4 5 6
5.	Advisory Councils	0 1 2 3 4 5 6
6.	Staff	0 1 2 3 4 5 6
7.	Faculty members	0 1 2 3 4 5 6
8.	Personnel Office	0 1 2 3 4 5 6
9.	Student counselors	0 1 2 3 4 5 6
10.	Community/community organizations	0 1 2 3 4 5 6

0	1	2	3	4	5	6
Not at all	Shared comments	Recommended learn more about	Informally shared book(s), articles and notes on subject matter	Prepared a formal presentation, engaged in dialogue/discussion on the implications for your organization	Prepared a formal presentation that was given to a group	Prepared a formal presentation and took steps to implement an organizational change that came as a result to exposure to the institute session

indicated response. The other groups: presidents who did not attend, boards of trustees, advisory councils, personnel offices, student counselors, and community/community organizations received very sporatic ratings in terms of the total number of presidents who sought out these groups to share information with them.

The second part of question no. 3 requested that the participants indicate the degree to which information from the Institute was shared and or prepared for presentation to these ten groups or those groups in which they indicated they shared information with. The majority of responses centered around ratings of one, two, and three; information was for the most part informally shared with other groups. Within these three ratings, no. 3 received the highest number of responses; information from the institute was not only informally shared, but book(s), articles and their notes on the subject matter were also distributed. This was true also, for most participants. Ratings four, five, and six, however, did as a total number of participant ratings, almost equal the total count received by no. 3 on the scale. In other words, there were almost as many formal presentations given to institutional groups as there was informal discussions and or the distribution of materials on Institute subjects. The same did not hold true, however, for the three groups: attending presidents, management councils, and staff which received the largest total ratings for groups with which presidents' shared information with. The results were that more formal presentations were made to these three groups than was information informally discussed. In fact, there is a good indication that a portion of these presentations were specifically organized to bring about organizational change or were the initial step to implement change within the institution.

Question no. 4 asked participants to describe how they might go about their job differently as a result of their exposure to the new information they received at an Institute. Figure 4. represents the question and the rating scale that was used.

Figure 4

Question (4) in Formative Evaluation

4. Since attending the last Institute, is there anything in the way in which you go about your job which is different from your former way and which you believe results directly from your experience in the session?

Please explain: _____

_____

_____

_____

_____

The diversity of the responses was to be expected. Due to the nature and particualr competency levels indicated by each participant in the evaluation, the response would reflect the nature of the individual's need for change. Most of the responses could be termed affective in information content. Many responses began with such phrases as: "I am more receptive to new ideas"; "awareness of need to improve"; "I am very interested in"; and "I have begun to consider." There were, however, those who indicated an actual outcome which showed actions taken. They ranged from having completed their own research and plans are being put into action to initiate change to starting up of processes to review evaluation criteria and procedures.

Question no. 5 asked participants to further elaborate on actual outcomes of initiatives taken by them which resulted from their experience in an Institute. Figure 5. represents the question and the format that was used.

Figure 5

Question (5) in Formative Evaluation

5. Indicate by circling the appropriate number, your choice which best represents an actual outcome of an initiative you undertook that resulted from your experience in the last Institute session.

   1. Set up advisory group to investigate the implications for practice of some aspect of the subject matter from the last institute that was found important to my organization.

   2. Reviewed the current organization structure to identify areas needing change where the subject matter from the last session could provide answers and or direction for making that change.

   3. Made an actual change in own job performance and or some aspect of staff/ faculty which resulted in a direct improvement in operational methods, institutional policy, procedures or allocation of resources.

   For response number 3, please circle one or more of the above areas in which you found change to occur and provide explanation of that change.

   Please explain: _____

   _____

   _____

   4. Other: _____

The majority of responses indicated that no. 2 was the most common outcome for them. They principally reviewed the current organizational structure to identify areas needing change where the subject matter for the last session they attended provided some answers and or gave direction to them in making plans or change. Responses no. 3 and no. 4 did further help to explain what changes were being made and how the participants themselves were involved. Examples of these are:

> "I am having my staff member preparing to attend a seminar by Jim Hammons to improve our evaluation instruments."

> "I've begun to start activities so as to be ready when computer equipment becomes available."

> "We are rewriting our position descriptions to clarify responsibilities and to eliminate gaps in responsibility."

> "I will employ the administration to head up marketing efforts for college and coordinate all current marketing functions."

> "We are currently evaluating our own evaluations against those I received at the Institute."

Question no. 6 asking participants to suggest any way in which the Institute sessions, themselves, could be improved was almost without exception often left blank. Some of the responses that were given were regarding elements of planning and organizing an Institute which were for the most part, out of the hands of the Institute staff. The responses, however, should be noted:

> "Have your computer demonstration people prepared to demonstrate a system."

"The material given by the consultants was too much for the period of time available."

"This was a tough subject to make exciting."

"Continue bringing in top quality consultants. (This *was* something - we could control, however.)"

Question no. 7 asked participants to provide their own evaluation of the Institute and make comments regarding their experience. Figure 6. represents the question and the ratings that were used.

Figure 6

Question (5) in Formative Evaluation

7. Overall my evaluation of the last session I attended was:

0	1	2	3	4	5	6
Unfavorable			Expressed Interest			Very Favorable

Comments: _____

_____

_____

_____

Most ratings were within the range of four to six. Occasionally, a rating of one or two was expressed, but this was rare. Few comments were received regarding the individual's rating, but they are worth noting.

"We just didn't seem to ever get to finance."

"Monday night's presentor was much better than Sunday night's presentor."

Best we've had - filled my own needs."

In some cases, presidents would send one of their top administration or faculty to attend an Institute in their stead. One dean did return their formative evaluation with a personal story that is worth telling.

"Although I was a president's representative and not a president, I got a welcome response from those present which, as an outsider, I certainly appreciated. I was most impressed with the amount of material which was covered and the variety of the agenda. North Carolina State is providing a great service with this series."

Outcomes of Summative Evaluations

Upon completion of all 7 Institutes, presidents applying for graduation received summative evaluations. Below is a summary and review of feedback received from graduates. In particular, the quality of the guest researchers and practitioners that were brought in to conduct the sessions was the ultimate strength that made the biggest overall contribution to the presidents' learning experiences. Secondly, the quality of the topics discussed and the contribution to the management needs of presidents in operating their respective institutions was seen as being vital to their continued interest in upcoming planned sessions. Thirdly, there was a great deal of support for having experienced "outside" experts who brought with them information on events, activities and management strategies produced by other presidents and community college systems in other states. And finally, the format and organization of the Institute sessions was seen as being an important strength because it provided the environment which was conducive for learning.

The design of the current Institute, however, was not without its faults as a model for planned leadership development. Presidents responding to suggest revisions in the model, however, only had two major changes they would like to see happen. One, they would like to have only 3 or 4 Institute sessions per year and two, they would like to have them scheduled, in advance, of their planned yearly activities so that they could attend all of the planned sessions. Often, it was described, there was too much conflict between planned session dates and other critical activities (i.e., trustee meetings, commission hearings).

Looking at the seven Institutes in review, the presidents were asked what they saw as being the future need of the community college system for a program for leadership development. The response to this was almost a total agreement among participants that there exists a "critical need" for such a program. Although some felt or saw the need as less than at the critical stage, it was agreed that a prevailing demand exists for leadership development for current and future leaders.

Due to a foreseen demand for leadership development in a planned program, the presidents suggest several major issues or topics they felt should receive priority should another Institute be offered. These are the suggested topics:

(1) Faculty and staff evaluations
(2) Impact research and outcomes assessment
(3) Marketing
(4) Long range planning for curriculum, facilities and personnel
(5) Developing linkages with high schools
(6) Budget management
(7) Survival in the next 11 years, how to offset the decline in traditional student populations

Professional Development - Who's Responsibility Is It?

With everything that has come out of the Presidents' Institute, the experiences, the recognition, the impact on the competencies of presidents, there is still the question to what extents should this type of professional development be the responsibility of the individual, the community college, the Department of Community Colleges, and the university? Should all be responsible or only one source and to what degree should each source be financially responsible to absorb the cost of leadership program(s)? Asked to respond to these questions, the presidents essentially could not form a consensus on the answers. Several major outcomes of their responses are important to note. No one believed the individual should pay the full cost for leadership development. However, at some point the individual should pay for some of the cost involved. Secondly, the individual institution was seen as being responsible for the full cost over and above any other source for financial support. Thirdly, it was felt that there could be a shared support between the four sources or a combination thereof, however, the institution once again, was seen as being responsible to pay the majority of the expense.

And lastly, asked to foresee their role as presidents who would be willing to pay the tuition cost of a self-supporting leadership program for new and emerging leaders, the majority of presidents responded that they would; half said they would pay the full cost and half said they would want the financial support of other sources to be included in the full payment.

CONCLUSION

"Innovative programs for leadership development are a form of uniqueness for community colleges as well."

Dick Alfred, speaking to the Presidents' Leadership Institute, 1984

The first Presidents' Leadership Institute as a model for future leadership development programs was a success. It embodied the human and material resources desired by the North Carolina community college president and it provided the needed information they require to be more effective practitioners. Based upon the experiences they had and the outcomes they experienced that were conveyed in their summative evaluations, the Presidents' Institute did, in fact, represent a viable model for future leadership programs.

At this time two things can be concluded. One, a model for a leadership development program has been tested and found to be an accepted program to implement. Secondly, there is a critical to high need for leadership development programs to be available to meet the growing demands of new and emerging leaders for professional development. What cannot be concluded, however, is who should take the first step towards commitment of financial resources to fund future leadership programs? Who will take the leadership role on this, the most pressing issue, is yet to be decided.

The role the Institute has played in becoming the nation's first, statewide leadership program for community college presidents will not only set precedent upon which future leadership programs will emerge but it will set a standard of excellence that extends through the institution where excellence in performance can be an opportunity shared by faculty, the administration, and most importantly, students.

Influences upon that leadership now more than ever challenge the role of the presidency to become a planner of life long education for the community, an analyst of local and national demographic trends, a knowledgeable user of computerized data systems, and a marketer of academic and economic outcomes whereby their institutions achieve status before legislative decision-makers.

All of this leads to a question of leadership ability. What can the presidential decision-maker do to contribute to their own skill development and standards of excellence in managing the organization? In part, this has been answered by the Institute. On the other hand, actual outcomes accrued to each president by their own participation do differ and it is for the reader to review these personal outcomes of the formative and summative evaluations to determine for themselves if the challenge to excellence can be achieved through a similar program for leadership development in their state.

In North Carolina, two positive steps have been taken to meet the challenge of leadership development. North Carolina State University in Raleigh, North Carolina has instituted a Management Development Certificate Program, a non-degree certificate program for life long education students. Many of the products of the

Institute this year will be worked into this program of study for participating students, many of whom hold mid-level management positions at their post-secondary institutions. Through cooperation between the Department of Adult and Community College Education and the Department of Political Science and Public Administration, the program will offer graduate-level credit for courses designed to upgrade and develop management skills and functions. Also transfer of these classes to masters and doctoral programs can be achieved upon successful admission to a selected program.

Important to the lead role established by North Carolina State University in instituting both the Presidents' Leadership Institute and the Management Development Certificate, is a resolution which was unanimously passed by the North Carolina Association of Public Community College Presidents urging the North Carolina Department of Community Colleges to work with the General Assembly in seeing the following resolutions made by the Association be acknowledged and implemented:

Whereas, leadership at the state and institutional levels is the key to ensuring quality and progress for the community college system; and

Whereas, the Community College Presidents' Leadership Institute was a pilot project to determine its feasibility as a model for leadership renewal; and

Whereas, the program not only contributed to the professional development of the chief executives participating, but has distinguished itself in being selected by the American Association of Community and Junior Colleges for publication of the proceedings to assist other colleges in their leadership development initiatives nationwide; and

Whereas, community colleges as teaching institutions need access to similar quality programs to develop their most important resource - their people;

Be It Therefore Resolved that the North Carolina Association of Public Community College Presidents commends the North Carolina State Board of Community Colleges and the Department of Community Colleges for their support of this project, further that special appreciation be extended to the Department of Adult and Community College Education, North Carolina State University, and to Dale F. Campbell, Project Director who conducted the Institute, for its significant contribution to the profession.

Be It Further Resolved that NCAPCCP requests that the North Carolina Department of Community Colleges work with the Department of Adult and Community College Education to develop and support a comprehensive leadership and faculty upgrading program utilizing the available resources of the Consolidated University system.

Because of the historically strong linkage between the North Carolina Department of Community Colleges, the North Carolina Association of Public Community College Presidents and North Carolina State University, the adoption of this resolution should have broad support and good success in being further implemented across the state. Moreover, with the success of the Presidents' Leadership Institute as a pilot project for leadership development, other states can now implement similar projects that will address the needs of their new and emerging leaders. Leadership renewal, too, cannot be overlooked as a vital component of a state by state effort to enhance opportunities for excellence in campus leadership.

To the current and future community of campus administrators, the challenge goes out to pioneer other statewide efforts to build the leadership of today's community, technical and junior colleges. At no time has the threat of institutional decline been more widespread than it is today in the 1980s. Yet there are many good reasons to believe that personal motivation and courage to strive for a better organization can and does exist within the internal and external constituency of all colleges today. Taking the lead in channeling this support for the good of the community college system is the challenge. Stimulating enthusiasm for great leadership is the goal.